Design Fundamentals with Canva

Dedication

This book is dedicated to all the aspiring designers, the creative souls who see the world through a lens of vibrant colors and captivating visuals. To those who dare to dream big, who transform ideas into stunning realities, and who believe that design has the power to communicate, inspire, and connect. This is for the individuals who find joy in the meticulous arrangement of type, the careful selection of color palettes, and the art of crafting compelling narratives through visual storytelling. This is for everyone who seeks to unlock their creative potential and master the art of design with confidence, making the world a more visually appealing place, one pixel, one line, and one carefully chosen font at a time. This is for those who are unafraid to experiment, to learn, and to grow, embracing the beauty and power of visual communication in all its forms, guided by the principles presented within these pages. It is a testament to the power of imagination, the limitless possibilities of digital creation, and the enduring human need to express ourselves through art. May this book serve as both inspiration and a practical guide on your journey.

Preface

In today's visually driven world, the ability to create compelling and effective designs is a highly sought-after skill. Whether you're a small business owner, a social media manager, an educator, or simply someone who wants to elevate their visual communication, mastering graphic design is more valuable than ever. This book aims to empower you to do just that, providing a friendly and accessible guide to unlocking the potential of Canva, a powerful yet intuitive design tool. This book is not just about learning to use the software; it's about understanding the fundamental principles of design – color theory, typography, layout, and visual hierarchy – and applying them effectively. We'll explore these concepts through clear explanations, practical examples, and step-by-step instructions, ensuring that you can confidently translate your ideas into polished, professional designs. We will cover everything from basic navigation and tool usage to advanced techniques, providing you with the knowledge and confidence to create stunning visuals for any purpose. From social media graphics to marketing materials and beyond, this book will equip you with the skills to create impactful designs that capture attention and effectively communicate your message. Get ready to unleash your inner designer and transform your visual communication!

Introduction

Welcome to the world of graphic design! This book serves as your comprehensive guide to mastering the art of visual communication using Canva, a remarkably user-friendly yet powerful design platform. Whether you're a complete beginner taking your first steps into the world of design, or you have some prior experience but want to enhance your Canva skills, this book is designed to meet your needs. We understand that learning graphic design can sometimes feel daunting, filled with technical jargon and complex concepts. That's why we've taken a different approach. Our goal is to make the learning process enjoyable, accessible, and most importantly, effective. We'll break down the fundamental principles of design into easy-to-understand terms and demonstrate how to apply them practically within the Canva interface. Throughout the book, you'll find numerous examples, tips, and tricks to maximize your Canva experience and avoid common design pitfalls. We'll cover a wide range of design projects, from creating eye-catching social media graphics and marketing materials to designing presentations and even basic website elements. By the time you finish this book, you'll not only possess the technical skills to use Canva proficiently but also a strong understanding of the underlying principles that drive effective design. So, let's begin this exciting journey into the world of design. Let's create something amazing together!

Understanding Canvas Interface and Features

Embarking on your Canva journey begins with understanding its intuitive interface. Canva's strength lies in its user-friendly design, making it accessible to both design novices and experienced professionals. The initial impression is one of clean organization and straightforward navigation, a crucial aspect for a design tool aiming for broad accessibility. This section will serve as your personalized tour, guiding you through the key elements and functionalities.

Upon logging in, you'll be greeted by the Canva dashboard, a central hub for all your design projects. This isn't just a blank page; it's a dynamic workspace, reflecting your recent creations, templates, and collaborative projects. [Insert screenshot of Canva dashboard here]. Notice the organized layout: Prominent sections guide you toward creating new designs, accessing your existing projects, and exploring the vast library of templates and resources. The left-hand navigation bar is your constant companion, providing quick access to crucial features.

Creating a new design is as simple as clicking the "Create a design" button. Here, you'll be presented with a comprehensive list of pre-set dimensions catering to various design needs – from social media posts to presentations, posters, and even custom sizing options. This eliminates the guesswork of correctly sizing your design for specific platforms, ensuring your visuals are perfectly optimized for their intended use. Selecting the correct dimensions at this initial stage is crucial for avoiding resizing issues later in the process. Choosing the wrong dimensions can lead to blurry or distorted images when published.

Once you select your preferred dimensions, Canva opens a new design workspace. This is where the magic happens. The interface is meticulously designed to provide easy access to all the necessary tools and elements. At the top, you'll find options for saving, sharing, and downloading your design. A search bar allows for quick access to templates, elements, and images within Canva's extensive library.

The left-hand sidebar houses the bulk of Canva's tools. It's the command center for all your design tasks. You'll find categories for elements such as text, images, shapes, lines, and videos, providing a well-organized selection for your design needs. Within each category, you can further refine your search, selecting specific styles or types of elements. This sidebar is constantly available, allowing you to seamlessly add and manipulate elements throughout your design process. [Insert screenshot of the Canva left sidebar here]. Notice the clear categorization and intuitive search functionality; this allows you to quickly find the assets you need, saving you valuable time and effort.

The image upload section deserves special attention. Canva allows you to seamlessly integrate your own images, ensuring your designs reflect your brand's specific visual language and personal touch. [Insert screenshot of the image upload section here]. The process is intuitive: you can drag and drop images directly from your computer or use the upload button to browse and select your files. Canva supports a wide range of image formats, providing flexibility in how you build your designs. It's important to note that high-resolution images are key to producing professional-looking designs. Avoid using low-resolution images as they can result in pixelation and a less-than-ideal final product.

The "Elements" panel provides an extensive library of pre-designed graphics, images, and icons. These elements are categorized by type and style, facilitating efficient browsing and selection. [Insert screenshot of the elements panel here]. From simple shapes and lines to complex illustrations and photos, the elements panel provides a wealth of visual assets that can significantly enhance the appeal and message of your designs. Remember that while using pre-designed elements can expedite your design process, maintaining consistency and a cohesive visual style is crucial. Overusing elements without a clear plan can lead to an overcrowded and visually cluttered final product.

Canva's templates are a powerful tool for both beginners and experienced designers. They provide pre-designed layouts that you can customize to match your specific needs. This means you don't have to start from scratch every time you begin a new project. Instead, you can select a template and adapt its elements to create a unique design. The templates are organized into categories based on their purpose and design style. [Insert screenshot of the templates section here]. This intuitive organization facilitates a quicker workflow, streamlining the process of creating engaging and visually appealing designs. The ability to easily modify templates allows for creative freedom while still adhering to the fundamental principles of effective design.

Understanding the layout and functionality of the design canvas is crucial for efficient workflow. The canvas acts as your primary workspace; it's where you arrange elements, text, and images to create your design. Notice how easily you can resize elements using the drag handles or manually inputting dimensions. Canva's intuitive drag-and-drop functionality simplifies the placement and repositioning of elements. This intuitive design ensures the process of placing and adjusting elements is as seamless as possible. It's important to note that effective use of white space and intentional placement of elements is crucial for creating a visually balanced and appealing design. Overcrowding your design can lead to confusion and reduced visual appeal.

Navigating the various panels and tools is straightforward, and Canva provides helpful tooltips and guidance when needed. Experimenting with different features is encouraged, as it's the best way to discover the full extent of Canva's capabilities. From subtle adjustments to bold design choices, Canva empowers you to take control of your creative vision and bring your ideas to life. The platform's intuitive design ensures that the process of exploring these features remains enjoyable and accessible. Don't hesitate to explore the various options and functionalities; the more familiar you become with the interface, the more effectively you can utilize Canva's capabilities.

Canva's file management system is equally user-friendly. Your designs are automatically saved, eliminating the risk of losing your progress. The organization tools allow you to easily name, categorize, and find specific projects. This feature is invaluable for managing multiple designs, especially as your design portfolio expands. The intuitive design of Canva's file management system significantly reduces the administrative workload involved in design projects, ensuring a more streamlined workflow. This eliminates the frustrating search for lost or misplaced files, freeing up more time for the creative process.

In conclusion, this guided tour offers a solid foundation for confidently using Canva. The platform's user-friendly interface and well-organized tools and features make it accessible to anyone, irrespective of their prior design experience. Mastering the interface is the first step toward unleashing your creative potential and creating stunning visuals. By actively exploring the features and familiarizing yourself with the workspace, you'll quickly become comfortable using this powerful tool. The ease of navigation and intuitive functionality ensures the focus remains on the creative process, allowing you to express your vision without being hampered by complex software. Remember to practice and experiment. The best way to learn Canva is by using it!

Core Design Principles Balance and Alignment

Now that we've explored Canva's interface, let's delve into the core principles of design that will elevate your creations from simple visuals to impactful masterpieces. These principles aren't just abstract concepts; they're the fundamental building blocks of effective communication through design. Understanding and applying them will significantly improve the visual appeal and effectiveness of your Canva projects. We will begin by examining the crucial concepts of balance and alignment.

Visual balance is the distribution of visual weight across a design. Think of it like a seesaw: you need to distribute the weight evenly to prevent it from tipping over. In design, this "weight" is determined by several factors, including the size, color, and complexity of elements. An unbalanced design feels unstable and can distract the viewer from your message. A balanced design, however, feels harmonious and naturally draws the eye across the composition.

There are three main types of balance: symmetrical, asymmetrical, and radial. Symmetrical balance, also known as formal balance, is the most straightforward. It involves creating a mirror image on either side of a central axis. Think of a classic logo with text mirrored on either side of a central emblem. This type of balance is very stable and often conveys a sense of formality, tradition, and order. It's frequently seen in corporate branding and formal announcements. In Canva, achieving symmetrical balance is as simple as mirroring elements across the canvas's center line. You can use Canva's duplicate feature to easily create mirrored elements and then make small adjustments to perfect the symmetry.

Let's illustrate this with a practical example. Imagine you're designing a promotional flyer for a law firm. A symmetrical design, with the firm's logo centrally positioned and text mirroring across the vertical axis, would communicate professionalism and trustworthiness. The logo could be flanked by similar-sized images of the office building or a relevant legal symbol. Even the font size could be balanced, with larger headlines echoing each other on the opposing sides of the logo.

Asymmetrical balance, also known as informal balance, is more dynamic and less predictable than symmetrical balance. It achieves equilibrium by using elements of different visual weights strategically positioned on the page. A large element on one side can be balanced by several smaller elements on the other. This type of balance offers greater flexibility and visual interest, allowing for more creative freedom and often reflecting a modern and innovative sensibility. While it appears less structured, a well-executed asymmetrical design is just as effective at capturing the viewer's attention and communicating its message.

Consider designing a travel brochure showcasing exciting adventure activities. A large, captivating image of a mountain climber on one side could be balanced by several smaller, strategically placed images and text blocks on the opposite side, each contributing to the overall sense of adventure. The size and visual impact of the climber's photo are counterbalanced by the cumulative effect of several smaller elements, creating a dynamic and engaging visual. The text sections could be distributed to strategically emphasize various aspects of the trip. A smaller image might show the resort, while text highlights prices and dates. This approach avoids monotony and creates a more engaging visual narrative.

Radial balance is less common but highly effective when used correctly. It centers the design around a single point, with elements radiating outwards from that central point like spokes on a wheel. This creates a strong visual focus and often conveys a sense of movement, energy, or unity. Think of a mandala or a fireworks display – these are classic examples of radial balance. In Canva, you can achieve radial balance by arranging elements in concentric circles or using radiating lines to guide the viewer's eye to the central point.

A fantastic application of radial balance in Canva would be the design of a birthday invitation. The central point could be a large, stylized number representing the age being celebrated, and elements such as colorful images or decorative patterns could radiate outwards from this number, creating an eye-catching and festive invitation. Even the text could subtly reflect the radiating pattern, with progressively shorter lines or different font sizes creating a visually appealing flow.

Once you have established balance, alignment is crucial for ensuring readability and a pleasing visual hierarchy. Alignment refers to the way elements are positioned in relation to each other. Consistent alignment provides visual order and improves readability, making your designs more easily understood. Canva offers powerful alignment tools, making it simple to align elements to the left, right, center, or top and bottom. Use these tools diligently to maintain consistency in your design.

Consider the impact of misaligned text and images. Inconsistent alignment creates a messy and unprofessional appearance, making it difficult for the viewer to scan and comprehend the information. A well-aligned design, on the other hand, guides the viewer's eye smoothly through the layout, ensuring your message is effectively communicated. The visual cues created by alignment enhance the overall aesthetic appeal and emphasize the importance of specific elements.

Let's imagine you are designing a website banner. Using Canva's alignment tools, you could neatly align your headline text to the center, creating a strong visual focus. Then, align supporting text to the left to maintain a clean layout and good readability. You could further improve the design by strategically aligning images and icons within the layout, ensuring that they don't clash with the text and maintain a coherent visual flow.

Without proper alignment, the banner would appear disjointed, making it difficult to read the information presented. Imagine the headline placed slightly off-center, with image captions at different alignments. This would immediately create a negative visual impact, distracting the viewer from the content and undermining the overall effectiveness of the design.

The use of grids is a powerful technique to enhance alignment. While not explicitly featured as a tool in Canva's standard interface, you can achieve the effect of a grid by visually guiding the arrangement of elements. Think of imagining a subtle grid structure underlying your design canvas. Using guides or rulers can be extremely helpful here. This allows you to place elements with precision, ensuring a balanced and well-aligned layout. This invisible grid helps to create a sense of order and consistency, even in designs that are not strictly symmetrical or formal.

In conclusion, mastering balance and alignment is crucial for creating visually appealing and effective designs in Canva. By understanding the different types of balance and actively using Canva's alignment tools, you can create professional-looking designs that effectively communicate your message and leave a lasting impression on your audience. Experiment with these principles; practice is key to understanding how to use them to elevate the quality of your designs to a professional level. Remember to frequently review and refine your work; ensuring a constant check for balance and alignment will yield much better results. By incorporating these design fundamentals into your workflow, you'll transform your Canva creations into visually compelling and engaging communications.

Understanding Color Theory and its Application

Now that we've established the foundational principles of balance and alignment, let's move on to a crucial aspect of design: color theory. Color is more than just a visual element; it's a powerful tool that evokes emotions, conveys messages, and shapes the overall impact of your design. Understanding color theory will allow you to make conscious and effective color choices in Canva, transforming your designs from merely acceptable to truly captivating.

The cornerstone of color theory is the color wheel. This circular arrangement of colors displays the relationships between hues, showing how they interact and create different effects. The most common color wheel is based on the RYB (Red, Yellow, Blue) primary color model, although the RGB (Red, Green, Blue) model, used extensively in digital design, is also important to understand. Understanding the RYB model is helpful for understanding traditional mixing techniques, while RGB is crucial for working with digital tools like Canva.

Within the color wheel, we identify primary colors (Red, Yellow, Blue in RYB; Red, Green, Blue in RGB), which cannot be created by mixing other colors. Secondary colors are created by mixing two primary colors (Green, Orange, and Purple in RYB; Cyan, Magenta, Yellow in RGB). Tertiary colors are formed by mixing a primary and a secondary color. These color relationships provide the basis for understanding various color harmonies.

One of the most common and effective color harmonies is complementary color. Complementary colors lie directly opposite each other on the color wheel. They create high contrast and visual excitement. Think of the vibrant pairing of red and green, or blue and orange. In Canva, you can easily find complementary colors using the color picker tool; simply select one color and the tool will highlight its complement. However, using pure complementary colors at full saturation can sometimes be overwhelming. Consider using muted versions or varying the saturation to create a more balanced and sophisticated effect. For example, instead of a harsh bright red and green, opt for a muted burgundy paired with a sage green for a more refined aesthetic.

Analogous colors sit next to each other on the color wheel, creating a harmonious and calming effect. They often share similar undertones, leading to a visually cohesive design. For instance, using shades of blue, teal, and green creates a soothing and tranquil atmosphere, perfect for designs related to nature, serenity, or relaxation. Analogous color schemes offer a visually pleasing and less jarring effect than complementary colors, making them ideal for brand identities that want to project a sense of calm and consistency. Consider a spa brand using muted greens, blues, and light grays, conveying a message of relaxation and tranquility.

Triadic color harmonies use three colors evenly spaced around the color wheel, forming an equilateral triangle. This combination creates a vibrant and visually striking effect, balancing the energy of complementary colors with the harmony of analogous colors. A classic example is a triadic scheme using yellow, blue, and red. However, choosing the right shades and saturations is crucial to avoid a jarring visual effect; using pastel shades of these colors would create a far softer effect. Triadic color schemes are highly versatile and can be used across a wide array of design projects, from websites to marketing materials. Imagine a children's book using bright yellow, teal, and red to convey playfulness and energy.

Beyond these fundamental harmonies, there are other color schemes to explore, including tetradic (four colors forming a rectangle on the color wheel) and split-complementary (a base color paired with the two colors adjacent to its complement). Experimentation is key; the beauty of Canva is in its flexibility and the opportunity to explore these various color schemes.

Beyond the technical aspects, color psychology plays a vital role in design. Different colors evoke distinct emotions and associations. Red is often associated with energy, passion, and urgency; blue with calmness, trust, and stability; green with nature, growth, and serenity; yellow with optimism, joy, and creativity; and purple with royalty, luxury, and wisdom. Understanding these psychological associations enables you to make strategic color choices that align with your design's purpose and target audience. A company promoting eco-friendly products might use calming greens and blues, whilst a technology startup might use vibrant blues and oranges to signal innovation and dynamism.

Canva offers various tools to help you select and apply colors. The color picker allows you to choose colors from an image or create custom colors using hex codes, RGB values, or HSL sliders. You can also create and save your custom palettes, ensuring consistency across your projects. Canva's pre-designed templates often include thoughtfully curated color palettes that you can adapt to your needs. However, remember that the default palettes are simply a starting point; customizing them according to your branding requirements or the feeling you wish to elicit in your design will make your work stand out.

When implementing color theory in Canva, consider your brand's identity. If your brand is associated with luxury, a sophisticated color palette incorporating deep purples, golds, or rich blacks might be appropriate. If it's a youthful and energetic brand, brighter colors and bolder contrasts are likely to be more effective. The application of color must always be considered in relation to the message and the target audience.

Moreover, consider the context of your design. The color palette suitable for a wedding invitation would differ significantly from that of a construction company's brochure. Wedding invitations might call for softer pastels and romantic hues, while the construction company might benefit from a palette emphasizing strength and reliability, using earth tones and grays.

Remember that color is subjective and cultural factors also play a role in how colors are perceived. While certain color associations are generally accepted, always test your designs and gather feedback to ensure your color choices resonate with your target audience. A/B testing different color palettes can provide valuable insight into which colors are most effective in achieving your design goals.

Mastering color theory in Canva is an ongoing process, demanding continuous learning and experimentation. Don't hesitate to explore different color combinations, study successful designs, and analyze the color choices of established brands in your industry. By understanding the principles of color theory and using Canva's tools effectively, you'll be able to create visually impactful designs that communicate your message powerfully and effectively. Your designs will not only be aesthetically pleasing but also strategically aligned with your communicative goals. The ability to consciously select and use color is a skill that will significantly enhance your overall design capabilities.

Typography Choosing and Using Fonts Effectively

Having explored the captivating world of color theory, we now turn our attention to another cornerstone of effective design: typography. Typography, the art and technique of arranging type, is far more than just choosing a pretty font; it's about creating legible, visually appealing, and communicative text that enhances your overall design. In Canva, mastering typography is crucial for transforming your designs from visually cluttered to elegantly composed.

Understanding the basics of font families and typefaces is your first step. Font families are groups of fonts that share a common design, including variations in weight (light, regular, bold), style (italic, condensed), and width. For example, Times New Roman is a font family, encompassing various weights and styles. Within a font family, each individual variation is known as a typeface. Thus, Times New Roman Bold Italic is a typeface within the Times New Roman font family. Choosing the right typeface from the right font family is essential for maintaining visual consistency and readability in your designs.

Readability is paramount. A visually stunning font might look fantastic on its own, but if it's difficult to read, it undermines your design's purpose. Factors affecting readability include font size, font weight, line spacing (leading), letter spacing (tracking), and kerning (the spacing between individual letter pairs). Canva provides easy-to-use tools to adjust these parameters. For example, you can adjust leading to optimize vertical spacing between lines and avoid text blocks that appear cramped or too airy. Similarly, tracking allows you to adjust the overall spacing between letters, which is essential for improving readability in all caps text, where letters can often appear clustered. Precise kerning, while more time-consuming, ensures that individual letter pairs look visually balanced, improving the overall aesthetic of your text.

Consider your target audience and the context of your design when selecting fonts. A formal invitation will demand a different typographic approach than a casual social media post. A formal invitation might benefit from a classic serif typeface like Garamond or Times New Roman, conveying elegance and sophistication. These typefaces, with their small flourishes at the ends of strokes, have a traditional and authoritative feel, making them well-suited for formal documents or invitations. In contrast, a social media post might call for a clean sans-serif typeface like Helvetica or Arial, ensuring readability across various screen sizes and contributing to a modern and approachable aesthetic. Sans-serif typefaces, characterized by their lack of flourishes, are frequently used in contemporary design for their clean and versatile nature.

Font pairings are equally important. Combining different fonts effectively enhances visual interest and hierarchy, guiding the reader's eye through your design. Avoid pairing fonts that are too similar; the resulting lack of contrast will make your text appear monotonous and less engaging. On the other hand, pairing fonts that clash aesthetically can overwhelm the reader. Strive for a balance, choosing fonts with complementary qualities, such as pairing a serif typeface with a sans-serif typeface, a script typeface with a sans-serif typeface, or a display typeface with a serif typeface. The goal is a visual harmony, not a visual battle.

For instance, a sophisticated pairing might involve a classic serif typeface like Georgia (for body text) coupled with a bold, clean sans-serif typeface like Montserrat (for headings). Georgia's readability and elegance, combined with Montserrat's modern feel and impact, would create a visually pleasing and hierarchical text structure. Conversely, for a more playful and informal feel, you could pair a playful script font like Pacifico (for accents) with a clean, geometric sans-serif like Lato (for main body text). Experiment with different combinations in Canva, using its built-in font library to test and refine your choices.

Visual hierarchy, achieved through effective typography, guides the reader's eye, emphasizing key information and providing a clear structure to your design. This hierarchy is often established by varying font sizes, weights, and styles. Large, bold headings draw immediate attention, while smaller, lighter body text provides supporting detail. Canva's text tools make it effortless to adjust these parameters, allowing you to effortlessly create a clear and intuitive visual hierarchy that will enhance the overall user experience.

However, remember that visual hierarchy is not solely reliant on font size; it also extends to color and placement. A strategically placed heading in a contrasting color will further enhance readability and direct the reader to your most important information. Experiment with color and positioning alongside typography to enhance this effect.

Beyond the visual aspects, consider the emotional impact of your font choices. Different fonts evoke different feelings. A playful script font can convey a sense of fun and whimsy, whereas a bold sans-serif font can communicate strength and authority. A delicate serif font can suggest elegance and sophistication. These associations must be considered carefully to ensure that your typography is consistent with the message you intend to communicate. The right font choice will reinforce your message, and the wrong one can subtly undermine it.

Canva's tools provide further assistance in optimizing your typography. The text editor allows for easy adjustments to font size, weight, color, spacing, and alignment. The ability to directly adjust kerning allows you to fine-tune the visual appearance of the text, ensuring that individual letters flow seamlessly together, enhancing the overall aesthetic impact. Canva also offers pre-designed text templates, which serve as valuable starting points for creating visually appealing text blocks. These templates demonstrate effective font combinations and text arrangements, proving a useful source of inspiration as you refine your design skills.

In addition to choosing the right fonts, consider accessibility. Choose fonts with high readability and sufficient contrast between text and background color to ensure that your designs are accessible to users with visual impairments. Canva offers tools to help check the contrast ratio of your text, ensuring your designs meet accessibility standards.

Mastering typography in Canva is an iterative process requiring careful consideration of font choice, readability, hierarchy, emotional impact, and accessibility. Experimentation is key to developing your typographic skills and creating designs that are not just visually appealing but also clearly and effectively communicate the intended message. Through careful selection and application of fonts, you can transform your designs from the ordinary to the extraordinary, capturing the attention of your audience and leaving a lasting impression. Your ability to use typography effectively will markedly enhance your design capabilities and significantly improve the impact of your visual communication. Remember to constantly study existing designs and experiment with new font pairings and layouts. This ongoing process will contribute towards a continual refinement of your design skills and broaden your ability to deliver strong, clear, and effective visual communication.

Creating Effective Layouts and Composition

Now that we've explored the nuances of color theory and typography, let's delve into the crucial aspect of layout and composition. A well-designed layout is the foundation of any successful visual communication, whether it's a simple social media post or a complex marketing brochure. Canva, with its intuitive drag-and-drop interface and extensive design elements, provides the perfect platform to experiment with and master these principles. Creating effective layouts isn't about arbitrary placement; it's about understanding fundamental design principles and applying them strategically to guide the viewer's eye and convey your message effectively.

One of the most fundamental concepts in layout design is the rule of thirds. This principle suggests that an image should be imagined as divided into nine equal parts by two equally-spaced horizontal lines and two equally-spaced vertical lines, and that important compositional elements should be placed along these lines or their intersections. This creates a more visually appealing and dynamic composition than simply centering everything. In Canva, you can easily visualize this grid by enabling the grid overlay in the settings. This allows you to consciously position your elements—images, text blocks, or other design elements—along these lines to achieve a naturally balanced and engaging composition. Imagine, for example, placing the main focal point of a travel brochure—a stunning photograph of a beach—at one of these intersections. The placement guides the viewer's eye effortlessly through the rest of the elements, making the brochure more visually pleasing and enhancing its overall effectiveness.

The golden ratio, another powerful compositional tool, is a mathematical ratio that appears frequently in nature and art. Approximated by 1.618, this ratio creates a sense of harmony and visual balance. While not as directly applicable in Canva's interface as the rule of thirds, understanding the golden ratio helps you make intuitive design choices. For instance, you can use the ratio to determine the proportions of different elements within your design, ensuring a harmonious and aesthetically pleasing arrangement. This could involve setting the width and height of an image based on the golden ratio or proportioning text blocks according to this principle. The result is a more visually satisfying and balanced layout than one created without considering this mathematical principle. The subtle difference it makes is often the key to transitioning from an 'okay' design to a truly exceptional one.

Beyond these abstract principles, practical application is key. Consider the purpose and platform of your design. A social media graphic needs a completely different layout strategy than a multi-page brochure. Social media posts often benefit from a clean, minimalist approach with a strong visual focal point to grab attention immediately. The short attention span inherent in social media necessitates a concise and impactful design. A brochure, on the other hand, can allow for more complex layouts with multiple sections, incorporating varying levels of hierarchy and visual weight. Understanding your audience and the platform will dictate the style of layout you utilize and the visual elements you incorporate. For example, while a densely-packed brochure might be acceptable, a similarly dense social media post will likely be overwhelming to the viewer.

Let's examine some specific examples. Consider designing a brochure for a local bakery. Using the rule of thirds, you might place a high-quality image of freshly baked bread in the top left intersection of the grid, drawing the viewer's attention immediately. Subsequent elements, such as the bakery's logo, address, and special offers, can then be strategically placed along other gridlines, guiding the reader's eye through the information smoothly and logically. Avoid placing crucial elements in the dead center; this often results in a static and uninteresting layout. The judicious use of whitespace also plays a crucial role here. Negative space, the area around your elements, prevents your design from appearing overcrowded, enhancing readability and making the information more digestible.

Conversely, an ineffective brochure layout might cram all information into the center, creating a cluttered and confusing visual experience. This dense arrangement overwhelms the viewer, making it difficult to discern key information. Imagine trying to read a wall of text without any visual breaks or hierarchy; the result is overwhelming and unproductive. Similarly, a poorly-designed social media post might feature multiple elements vying for attention, creating a visually chaotic and unappealing image that fails to communicate its message effectively. Such designs often fail to capture the viewer's attention, leading to a lost opportunity to engage with your audience.

For a website banner, a horizontal layout emphasizing the visual aspect often works best. A large, captivating image dominating the upper portion, accompanied by concise and impactful text beneath, can be far more successful than a crowded design with multiple conflicting elements. This clean arrangement draws the viewer's eye and allows them to quickly grasp the essence of the message. The choice of fonts—a larger, bold font for the main message and a smaller, supporting font for the secondary information—further enhances readability and ensures a coherent visual hierarchy.

Consider a website landing page that requires a more detailed presentation. Here, a layout that incorporates vertical sections, each with its own visual focus and clear messaging, becomes advantageous. A strong visual element might introduce each section, followed by concise text, call-to-action buttons, and other relevant elements, ensuring that the page is easy to navigate and that information is delivered logically and clearly. This organized structure guides the user through the page, improving their overall experience and maximizing their engagement.

Canva's templates provide excellent starting points for various design scenarios. While these templates offer pre-designed layouts, remember to customize them to reflect your brand and your specific message. Don't be afraid to experiment, adjust spacing, reposition elements, and refine the overall composition. The beauty of Canva lies in its flexibility and its ease of use, allowing you to iterate and refine your designs until they perfectly convey your intended message.

The creation of balanced and visually appealing layouts is an iterative process. It involves constant experimentation and refinement, informed by a solid understanding of fundamental design principles. Don't be afraid to try different approaches; look at successful examples from various platforms and analyze what makes them effective. By utilizing the rule of thirds, the golden ratio, and other compositional strategies, along with a keen eye for detail and an understanding of your target audience and platform, you can master the art of layout and elevate your designs from ordinary to extraordinary. Mastering Canva's features and functionalities allows you to implement these principles effortlessly, providing you with the tools to create stunning visuals that will capture the attention of your audience and successfully communicate your message. Remember, a strong layout is not just aesthetically pleasing; it's a crucial component of effective visual communication. The effort you put into achieving balance and harmony will directly translate into the impact and effectiveness of your designs.

Working with Images Editing and Optimization

Now that we've established the fundamentals of layout and composition, let's turn our attention to another crucial element of successful graphic design: image selection and optimization. High-quality images are the backbone of any compelling visual, and Canva provides a robust suite of tools to enhance and refine them. This section will guide you through the process of selecting, editing, and optimizing images within Canva, transforming ordinary pictures into powerful visual assets.

The first step in maximizing the impact of your images is to choose high-resolution sources. A blurry or pixelated image, no matter how well-composed the overall design, will detract from its professionalism and credibility. Avoid using images directly from a Google search; while convenient, these images often lack the resolution necessary for high-quality prints or digital displays. Instead, opt for professional stock photography sites (many offer free options), or use your own high-resolution images captured with a good quality camera. Canva itself offers a vast library of royalty-free images, many of which are free to use, saving you the hassle of sourcing them elsewhere. Understanding the difference between a low-resolution and high-resolution image is key. A low-resolution image will appear blurry or pixelated when enlarged, while a high-resolution image retains its sharpness and detail, even at larger sizes.

Within Canva, you'll find a range of tools to manipulate and enhance your images. The cropping tool allows you to remove unwanted portions of an image, focusing attention on the most visually appealing or relevant aspects. Careful cropping can significantly improve the overall composition, directing the viewer's gaze to the central subject. For example, a poorly-composed photograph featuring a distracting background can be dramatically improved by cropping to isolate the subject and eliminate visual clutter. Experiment with different cropping ratios to find the most effective composition. Canva often suggests optimal aspect ratios based on the design type, ensuring your image fits perfectly within the canvas.

Adjusting brightness and contrast is another crucial step in image optimization. A poorly lit image can appear dull and lifeless, whereas a well-adjusted image appears vibrant and engaging. Canva's intuitive brightness and contrast sliders allow you to fine-tune these parameters easily. Experiment with subtle adjustments until you achieve the desired visual effect. Over-adjusting can lead to an unnatural or washed-out look, so proceed cautiously. It is often helpful to compare your adjusted image to the original to assess the impact of your changes. The goal is to enhance the image, not distort it.

Canva also offers a variety of filters to modify the overall mood and tone of your images. These filters apply pre-set adjustments to brightness, contrast, saturation, and other parameters, providing a quick way to change the image's aesthetic. From vintage effects to modern enhancements, Canva's filters provide ample options for enhancing your visuals. However, remember that less is often more. Overusing filters can result in an artificial or unnatural appearance, detracting from the overall quality of the design. Choose filters that complement the overall aesthetic of your project and avoid overwhelming the image with excessive effects. Experimentation is key, but strive for a refined, natural look rather than overly stylized enhancements.

Beyond basic adjustments, Canva allows for more advanced image editing techniques. Tools for adjusting saturation, sharpness, and hue provide a fine level of control over your images. These tools allow you to tweak color intensity, enhance details, and refine specific color tones, resulting in a more polished and visually appealing outcome. However, it's crucial to use these tools judiciously. Excessive manipulation can lead to an unnatural or artificial look, so make subtle changes to achieve the desired effect. These tools are particularly helpful for correcting issues like color casts or enhancing details in images that may have been slightly under-exposed or over-exposed during capture.

Consider the specific application of your image. An image for a website banner requires a different approach than one for a printed brochure. Website images benefit from compression to ensure fast loading times. Canva automatically optimizes images for web use, but understanding this concept will help you select and prepare the right image from the start. For print, high-resolution images are essential to avoid pixelation. Always check the resolution requirements for your intended output. Canva's exporting options allow you to choose different file formats and resolutions based on your intended use.

Let's illustrate with examples. Imagine you're designing a promotional banner for a new product launch. You've chosen a high-resolution image of the product against a clean background. Using Canva's cropping tool, you carefully remove any unnecessary elements, focusing on the product itself. Then, you adjust the brightness and contrast to enhance the vibrancy of the colors, ensuring the product stands out. Finally, you apply a subtle filter to give the image a more polished and professional look. This systematic approach transforms a good image into a truly compelling visual that effectively showcases your product.

Now, consider a different scenario: creating a social media post for a travel agency. You've chosen a stunning landscape photograph, but the sky is slightly overexposed. Canva's brightness and contrast tools enable you to subtly reduce the brightness of the sky, balancing it with the rest of the image. Then, using the saturation tool, you enhance the colors of the landscape, making it more vibrant and eye-catching. The final result is a visually arresting image that perfectly captures the essence of travel and adventure.

Finally, let's address the challenges of working with images that aren't ideal. Sometimes, the only image you have available may be of low resolution. While you can't magically increase its resolution, you can mitigate its drawbacks. Avoid enlarging the image too much, as this will only exacerbate the pixelation. Instead, use it strategically, perhaps as a smaller element within a larger design, or apply a filter to soften its appearance. Cropping can also help by focusing on the least pixelated areas. This strategic use minimizes the impact of the image's imperfections.

Remember to always respect copyright when using images. Canva's library provides a wealth of royalty-free options, but if using images from elsewhere, ensure you have the necessary permissions to avoid legal issues. Always attribute the source appropriately when required. This is crucial for maintaining ethical and legal compliance in your designs. Canva's built-in features even assist with this, allowing you to easily cite the source of your images.

In conclusion, mastering Canva's image editing tools is essential for creating impactful and professional designs. By understanding how to select, edit, and optimize images, you can elevate the quality of your work significantly. The techniques discussed in this section – from basic cropping and brightness adjustments to more advanced color correction and filter application – are fundamental to effective visual communication. Remember, the goal is not merely to edit images, but to enhance them, transforming them into powerful tools that effectively convey your message and leave a lasting impression on your audience. With practice and experimentation, you'll become adept at using Canva's image tools to create visually stunning and compelling designs.

Utilizing Shapes Lines and Icons

Building upon our exploration of image optimization, we now delve into the equally crucial elements of shapes, lines, and icons within Canva. These seemingly simple tools are incredibly powerful in shaping the visual narrative and enhancing the impact of your designs. Mastering their application is key to creating professional and visually appealing graphics.

Let's begin with shapes. Canva offers a vast library of pre-designed shapes, ranging from simple geometric forms like squares, circles, and triangles to more complex, customisable options. These aren't merely decorative elements; they serve a significant structural and communicative purpose. Consider using shapes to create compelling backgrounds. Instead of a plain white or solid-color backdrop, experiment with subtle gradients created using overlapping shapes or using shapes to frame specific elements within your design. A strategically placed semi-transparent shape can draw the eye to a key piece of text or image, creating a visually arresting focal point.

The versatility of shapes extends beyond backgrounds. They can act as containers for text, creating visually distinct sections within your design. For instance, you could enclose a call to action in a brightly colored, rounded rectangle to make it stand out from the surrounding content. Similarly, shapes can be used to visually separate different sections of a document or presentation. Imagine using a series of interconnected shapes to visually represent a flowchart, each shape representing a step in a process. This approach not only provides visual interest but also enhances understanding and information retention. Don't underestimate the impact of shape on the overall mood and feel of your design. Sharp, angular shapes often convey a sense of modernity and energy, while softer, rounded shapes communicate a more friendly and approachable atmosphere.

The strategic use of color in conjunction with shapes significantly impacts the overall visual appeal. Consider using contrasting colors to make certain shapes stand out, or using similar colors to create a sense of visual harmony. Experiment with different combinations to see what works best for your particular design. Don't be afraid to play with transparency; partially transparent shapes can add depth and visual interest without obscuring the underlying content. The layering feature in Canva allows you to arrange shapes in different layers, creating depth and visual complexity. Mastering the art of layering shapes will enhance your ability to create visually rich and layered designs.

Next, let's explore the power of lines. Often overlooked, lines are surprisingly versatile tools in graphic design. They can serve as guides for the eye, directing the viewer's attention to specific areas of the design. For instance, a subtle line can subtly connect elements that are thematically linked, creating a visual pathway through the design. Think of lines not just as straight edges but as flowing, dynamic elements. Consider using curved lines to create a sense of fluidity and movement, conveying a softer, more organic aesthetic. Alternatively, bold, straight lines can create a sense of order and structure, perfect for more formal designs.

Vary the thickness and style of your lines to create visual interest and hierarchy. Thin lines are often used for subtle division or emphasis, while thicker lines can create bolder visual dividers or draw attention to specific sections. Experiment with different line styles, such as dashed, dotted, or double lines, to add visual texture and complexity. The choice of line style should complement the overall aesthetic of your design, reflecting the tone and message you aim to convey. A minimalist design may benefit from simple, thin lines, while a more energetic design might benefit from bolder, more varied linework.

Lines can also be used to create visual frames or borders for text or images. Consider using a thin, subtle line to create a delicate frame around an image, or use a thicker, more prominent line to draw attention to a key piece of text. The strategic use of lines in this manner can subtly enhance the overall sophistication and polish of your design. Remember to consider the relationship between lines and the surrounding elements in your design. Lines should support and enhance the overall composition rather than compete with or distract from it.

Finally, let's consider the significant role of icons in Canva design. Icons are small, symbolic images that represent specific concepts or ideas. They are incredibly useful for adding visual interest and conveying information quickly and effectively. Canva offers a wide array of icons, categorized for easy navigation and selection. When choosing icons, consider the overall aesthetic of your design. Ensure that the icon style is consistent with the overall tone and visual language of your project.

Icons are particularly useful in situations where you want to convey information concisely and efficiently, such as in infographics or social media posts. A well-chosen icon can immediately communicate a complex idea, saving valuable space and enhancing understanding. For example, using an icon representing a telephone immediately communicates contact information, while an icon representing a calendar might clearly denote scheduled events or upcoming deadlines. The careful selection and placement of icons can significantly improve the readability and visual appeal of your designs. The use of icons can add a professional touch and improve the overall effectiveness of your communications.

Don't just randomly scatter icons throughout your design. Consider the relationship between icons and other elements, ensuring that the icons complement and enhance the overall design, rather than detracting from it. The placement of icons can guide the reader's eye and help to tell a story within the design. For instance, strategically placed icons can illustrate a timeline or map out a process, making the information clearer and more accessible.

In conclusion, mastering the use of shapes, lines, and icons in Canva is essential for creating visually appealing and impactful designs. These seemingly basic elements are incredibly powerful tools when used strategically. By understanding the principles of visual hierarchy, balance, and composition and applying these tools thoughtfully, you can transform ordinary designs into truly stunning and professional visual communications. Remember to experiment, iterate, and refine your designs until they effectively convey your message and engage your audience. Through careful planning and experimentation with Canva's extensive library of resources, you can harness the power of these simple tools to create designs that not only look professional but also effectively convey your intended message. The combination of these elements, alongside the image optimization techniques discussed previously, will allow you to create well-rounded, visually compelling designs that capture attention and communicate effectively.

Working with Text Formatting and Hierarchy

Now that we've explored the visual building blocks of Canva – images, shapes, lines, and icons – let's turn our attention to arguably the most crucial element of any design: text. Effective typography isn't just about choosing a pretty font; it's about crafting a clear, concise, and visually appealing message that resonates with your audience. Canva offers a robust set of tools to help you master this art, allowing you to create text-based designs that are both aesthetically pleasing and highly effective.

The foundation of effective text design lies in understanding the concept of visual hierarchy. Think of your design as a conversation; you want your audience to follow a clear path through the information you present. Visual hierarchy guides this path, directing the reader's eye to the most important information first. This is achieved primarily through the strategic use of text formatting: size, font, style, color, and spacing.

Let's start with font size. Larger text naturally draws more attention. This principle is fundamental to establishing hierarchy. Headlines, the most important piece of information, should be the largest. Subheadings, providing more detail, should be smaller than headlines, yet larger than the body text. The body text itself should be legible and comfortable to read, using a size appropriate for the intended viewing distance (consider whether your design will be viewed on a computer screen or a mobile phone). A consistently applied size hierarchy creates a smooth reading experience, guiding the eye effortlessly from one level of information to the next.

Next, consider font selection. Canva offers a wide array of fonts, each with its own personality and feel. Serif fonts (like Times New Roman or Garamond), with their small flourishes at the ends of letters, generally convey a more traditional and formal feel. Sans-serif fonts (like Arial or Helvetica), lacking these flourishes, are often perceived as more modern and clean. The choice of font should align with the overall tone and style of your design. A playful design might use a script font, while a professional report would benefit from a more conservative choice. However, it's crucial to avoid using too many different fonts within a single design. Sticking to a maximum of two, perhaps a headline font paired with a body text font, ensures visual harmony and prevents a cluttered appearance.

Beyond font choice, consider font styles. Bold, italic, and underlined text are all effective tools for creating emphasis. Use bolding for headlines and key phrases to immediately draw attention. Italics can be used for emphasis or to indicate quotations, while underlining should be used sparingly, as it can sometimes be less visually appealing compared to bolding. Consistent use of these styles reinforces your visual hierarchy and aids readability. Overuse, however, can lead to a cluttered and confusing design. Subtlety is key; use these formatting options strategically to draw attention to important information without overwhelming the reader.

Paragraph formatting is equally important. Consistent line spacing, indentation, and use of bullet points or numbered lists dramatically improve readability. Canva's built-in paragraph formatting tools allow you to adjust line height (leading), ensuring comfortable spacing between lines. Too much leading can make the text look sparse, while too little can make it feel cramped. Experiment with different settings until you find a balance that's easy on the eyes. Indentation can visually separate paragraphs, improving readability, particularly in longer text blocks. For longer texts, consider using bullet points or numbered lists to break up large blocks of text and improve comprehension. These formatting choices significantly influence the visual clarity of your designs, guiding the reader effectively through the information presented.

Color plays a crucial role in text hierarchy. The contrast between the text color and the background is essential for readability. Dark text on a light background is generally the most legible, while light text on a dark background can be effective in specific contexts, such as presentations or social media posts. However, always ensure sufficient contrast to avoid strain on the reader's eyes. Color can also be used to highlight specific text elements. A brightly colored call to action button, for example, can immediately grab the reader's attention and encourage engagement. But be mindful of color psychology; certain colors evoke specific emotions and associations. Use color strategically to enhance the emotional impact of your text, ensuring that it aligns with your overall design and message.

Creating effective text hierarchies is about more than just size and font choices; it's about creating a coherent and visually engaging flow of information. Consider how different text elements work together, ensuring that the hierarchy is intuitive and supports the overall message. For instance, a headline introduces the topic, subheadings break down the topic into smaller, more digestible chunks, and the body text provides further details. Call-to-action buttons are usually separate and visually distinct to motivate the reader to take a specific action.

Let's illustrate these principles with a practical example. Imagine you're creating a social media post advertising a workshop. Your headline, the most important element, might be "Master Canva in One Day!" in a bold, large, and visually striking font, perhaps a sans-serif font like Montserrat, in a vibrant color that stands out against the background image. Below, a subheading, perhaps in a slightly smaller size and a less bold font weight of the same font family, could read "Learn design principles and create stunning visuals." The body text, using a consistent and easily legible serif or sans-serif font, would contain specific details about the workshop's content, date, time, and registration link. Finally, a clear and prominent "Register Now!" button, perhaps in a contrasting color and a distinct shape, serves as a powerful call to action, guiding the reader to the next step.

Remember, consistency is paramount in text formatting. Maintain a consistent font family, size hierarchy, and color scheme throughout your design. This creates a cohesive and professional look, enhancing the overall impact of your message. Use Canva's built-in tools to easily adjust text alignment, spacing, and other formatting options. Experiment, play with different combinations, and iterate your designs until you achieve the desired level of visual clarity and impact. Effective typography is a fundamental skill for any designer, and by mastering Canva's text tools, you'll significantly enhance the quality and effectiveness of your visual communications. The ability to manage text formatting and visual hierarchy in Canva is a skill that will improve your design abilities significantly, ensuring that your messages are not only beautiful but easily understood and engaging. The combination of a visually pleasing and informative text layout will enhance your design's effectiveness.

The ability to effectively manipulate text within Canva is not simply about aesthetics. It's about crafting a clear and concise message that resonates with your audience. By understanding and implementing these principles of visual hierarchy and utilizing the versatile formatting tools within Canva, you can transform your designs from merely visually appealing to truly effective communications. Remember, the ultimate goal is to communicate your message clearly and persuasively, and skilled typography is the key to achieving this. Consistent practice and refinement of your skills will lead to designs that are both aesthetically pleasing and highly effective in communicating their intended message. Don't be afraid to experiment, constantly refining your approach until you achieve the perfect balance of visual appeal and clear communication.

Leveraging Canvas Templates and Design Elements

Canva's extensive library of templates and design elements significantly accelerates the design process, providing a foundation upon which you can build your unique creations. This section delves into the effective utilization of these resources, emphasizing efficient workflow techniques and practical strategies for customization.

Finding the right template is the first step. Canva categorizes its templates by design type – social media posts, presentations, flyers, posters, and more. Begin by identifying the purpose of your design. Are you creating a social media post for Instagram? A presentation for a business meeting? A marketing flyer for an event? Knowing this helps narrow down the search and saves valuable time. Once you've identified the design type, you can further refine your search using keywords related to your specific needs. For example, if you're designing a promotional flyer for a tech conference, you might search for "tech conference flyer," "technology event flyer," or similar terms. Canva's search functionality is remarkably robust, incorporating both textual and visual cues to match you with the most appropriate templates. Don't hesitate to browse through different categories and explore various design options; inspiration often comes from unexpected sources.

Once you've found a template that aligns with your vision, the process of customization begins. This is where your design skills and understanding of design principles come into play. Canva's intuitive interface allows for effortless modification. You can easily change colors, fonts, images, and layouts to perfectly reflect your brand identity and the message you wish to convey. Remember the principles of visual hierarchy discussed earlier: ensure the most important information remains prominently displayed, while secondary information is appropriately de-emphasized. Don't be afraid to experiment with different fonts and color palettes until you arrive at a combination that both visually appeals and effectively communicates your message.

Let's consider a practical example. Suppose you're creating an Instagram post announcing a new product launch. You find a template that has a clean, modern aesthetic and incorporates a striking image placeholder. Instead of simply replacing the placeholder image with your product photo, consider enhancing it further. Perhaps adding a subtle shadow or overlay to make it stand out more prominently. You might also adjust the font sizes and styles to match your brand's voice – a more playful font for a fun, youthful product or a more sophisticated font for a more premium offering. Experiment with color schemes to see what complements your product and brand best. A consistent color palette across all your marketing materials is essential for brand recognition and cohesiveness.

The power of Canva's templates lies not only in their pre-designed layouts but also in their adaptability. They provide a solid framework to avoid starting from scratch, allowing you to concentrate on the details and creative elements that bring your design to life. Don't feel constrained by the original template; use it as a starting point and let your creativity flow. Many templates include placeholder text, images, and icons. Replacing these with your own content, tailored to your specific needs, transforms a generic template into a unique and personalized design.

Canva's pre-made elements, including icons, illustrations, and graphics, further extend the possibilities of template customization. These elements enhance visual appeal and add depth to your designs. They provide a quick and easy way to incorporate visuals that convey specific concepts or emotions without the need to design them from scratch. For example, if your design involves highlighting speed and efficiency, incorporating an icon depicting a rocket or a speeding arrow can enhance the visual impact and clearly communicate your intended message. Similarly, if your design focuses on environmentally friendly products, you could include images of leaves, plants, or recycled materials. Remember, however, that less is often more; avoid overwhelming your design with too many elements. Choose those that directly support your message and enhance your overall design aesthetic.

Integrating these pre-made elements requires careful consideration of visual hierarchy. Ensure these elements don't detract from the primary message or create visual clutter. Consider the size, color, and placement of each element relative to the other design components. A well-placed icon or illustration can subtly enhance the overall impact of your design without overwhelming the viewer.

Let's illustrate this with another example: Imagine designing a marketing brochure for a new restaurant. You begin with a template featuring appealing layout options. Instead of merely replacing the placeholder photos with images of your restaurant's dishes, you carefully select high-quality, professional photographs that showcase the food in an appealing manner. You then select icons that represent key aspects of your restaurant's brand – perhaps a fork and knife for the food, a coffee cup for beverages, or a friendly chef icon to highlight the staff. These elements, carefully integrated into the existing template, subtly enhance the design and strengthen the message.

Efficient workflow is crucial when leveraging templates and elements. Begin by gathering all the necessary content – images, text, and branding materials – before starting the design process. Having this content readily available streamlines the workflow and prevents time-consuming searches during design. This pre-planning will significantly reduce the overall design time and maintain a consistent focus on the creative process.

Canva's features facilitate efficient workflow. For instance, the ability to save your work regularly ensures that you won't lose progress due to unexpected system shutdowns or interruptions. Utilize Canva's collaboration features to work efficiently with others on design projects, streamlining the design process and allowing for quick feedback and adjustments. Canva's brand kit function allows you to save your brand colors, fonts, and logos, ensuring a consistent brand image across all your projects.

Mastering Canva's templates and elements isn't merely about using pre-designed resources; it's about understanding how to effectively adapt and customize them to meet your specific needs. It's about transforming a generic framework into a unique and professional design that effectively communicates your message. By combining the efficiency of readily available resources with your own design skills and understanding of design principles, you can produce high-quality designs quickly and effectively. The key lies in thoughtful selection, meticulous customization, and a focus on efficient workflows, ensuring that every design element contributes to the overall effectiveness of the design. Through practice and experimentation, you'll develop an intuitive workflow that allows you to consistently produce stunning designs that effectively convey your message and leave a lasting impression on your audience. Remember, effective design isn't about simply using tools; it's about communicating a message clearly and persuasively.

Collaborating and Sharing Designs in Canva

Canva's collaborative features transform the design process from a solitary endeavor into a dynamic team effort, fostering seamless teamwork and efficient feedback loops. This collaborative aspect is particularly crucial for larger projects or when multiple perspectives are required to achieve the optimal design outcome. Understanding how to effectively utilize these features is vital for maximizing Canva's potential and streamlining your workflow.

The first step in collaborating on a Canva design is sharing it. This is achieved through a straightforward process within the Canva interface. Once you've created a design you want to share, locate the "Share" button, usually found in the upper right corner of the screen. Clicking this button opens a dialog box that allows you to specify who you wish to share the design with and what level of access they will have.

Canva offers a range of permission levels, allowing you to fine-tune the level of collaboration. The most common options include "Can view," "Can edit," and "Can comment." "Can view" grants recipients access only to view the design; they cannot make any changes. This is ideal for sharing a finished design with clients or stakeholders for their review. "Can edit" provides recipients with full editing privileges, enabling them to make changes, add elements, and modify existing components. This is suited for collaborative design projects where multiple team members contribute directly to the design's development. "Can comment" allows recipients to leave feedback directly on the design, similar to a digital proofing system. This is useful for gathering feedback before finalizing the design.

Choosing the correct permission level is crucial. Granting "Can edit" access to individuals who only require review may result in unintentional alterations. Conversely, restricting access to "Can view" for collaborators who need to actively contribute will hinder the workflow. Consider the role and responsibility of each collaborator before assigning permissions.

Let's consider a practical example: a marketing team designing a series of social media posts for a product launch. The team might consist of a designer, a marketing manager, and a copywriter. The designer would likely have "Can edit" access, enabling them to create and refine the design. The marketing manager might also have "Can edit" access to review the content and make strategic adjustments. The copywriter could have either "Can edit" access to make text modifications directly, or "Can comment" access to provide feedback on the messaging without altering the design itself. Each team member's role determines their required permission level.

Beyond assigning permissions, Canva facilitates collaborative workflows through real-time updates. Multiple users can work on the same design simultaneously, with changes reflected instantly for all collaborators. This real-time interaction fosters a dynamic and efficient design process, minimizing delays caused by waiting for design updates. Imagine a situation where a graphic designer is working on the visual aspects of a brochure while a copywriter simultaneously updates the text content. With Canva's real-time collaboration, both individuals can work concurrently, ensuring a seamless integration of text and visuals.

However, effective collaboration necessitates clear communication and coordinated efforts. Establishing a clear workflow from the outset is crucial to prevent conflicts or redundant work. Defining specific roles and responsibilities for each team member helps streamline the process, ensuring that everyone understands their contribution and avoids overlap. Regular communication through comments and direct messages within Canva keeps everyone informed of progress and allows for timely feedback.

Once the design is finalized, Canva provides various export options. You can export your design in several formats, including JPG, PNG, PDF, and even GIF formats, catering to diverse platforms and intended uses. The choice of format depends on where the design will be used. For instance, JPG is suitable for web use, while PNG retains transparency for logos or other elements requiring a transparent background. PDF is ideal for print media, ensuring high-quality reproduction. Consider the final destination of your design before selecting the appropriate export format.

Exporting in the correct format is critical for maintaining design integrity. Exporting a high-resolution image for print materials in a low-resolution format could lead to a pixelated and unprofessional outcome. Similarly, exporting a web-optimized design in a high-resolution format might unnecessarily increase file size and loading times.

Sharing the finished design is equally important. Canva offers multiple sharing methods. You can download the exported file and share it via email or file-sharing services. Alternatively, Canva allows for direct sharing links, enabling easy distribution to clients or colleagues without needing to download the file. The choice of sharing method depends on your preference and the recipient's requirements.

Effective collaboration extends beyond merely using Canva's sharing and permission features. It requires clear communication, defined roles, and a collaborative spirit among team members. Canva provides the tools, but the success of the collaborative effort depends on the team's approach. Regular check-ins, constructive feedback, and open communication are crucial for a successful collaborative design process. By utilizing Canva's collaborative features effectively and adopting a proactive approach to teamwork, you can significantly enhance the design process, leading to more efficient workflows and superior design outcomes. The result is a streamlined process that fosters creative synergy, resulting in more compelling and effective designs that accurately reflect the collective expertise and creativity of the entire team. The ability to seamlessly integrate diverse perspectives ensures a richer and more comprehensive design, maximizing the potential of every design project.

Designing Social Media Graphics for Various Platforms

Designing visually engaging social media graphics requires understanding the nuances of each platform. While Canva provides a user-friendly interface for creating these graphics, success hinges on adapting your design to the specific requirements and visual conventions of each social media network. Instagram, Facebook, Twitter, and LinkedIn, for example, each have distinct aesthetic preferences and technical specifications that will directly impact the effectiveness of your designs. Ignoring these platform-specific differences can lead to suboptimal results, reducing the impact of your marketing efforts.

Let's start with Instagram, a platform heavily reliant on visual storytelling. Instagram's users are drawn to high-quality images and videos. Therefore, your designs should prioritize visual appeal. Think about using vibrant colors, compelling imagery, and strong compositions. High-resolution images are crucial for crisp, clear presentation, especially on larger screens or when users zoom in. Consider the aspect ratio; while square images were once standard, Instagram now supports various aspect ratios, including vertical and horizontal formats, opening up more creative possibilities. Understanding which aspect ratio best suits your content is crucial to maximize its visual impact within the Instagram feed. A horizontally oriented image, for instance, might be best suited to showcasing landscapes or products in greater detail, while a vertically oriented image is commonly used for portrait-style content or emphasizing a specific element.

Instagram also thrives on short, engaging captions and relevant hashtags. While the visual aspect of your design is paramount, the text accompanying the image must be equally impactful and well-integrated. A visually stunning post paired with a poorly written or irrelevant caption can diminish its overall effectiveness. Consider using Canva's text tools to create visually appealing captions that complement the graphic's aesthetic. Experiment with different fonts, sizes, and colors to find a cohesive style. Ensure the text is easily readable against the background image, and remember to keep it concise to maintain user engagement.

Beyond individual posts, consider the importance of Instagram Stories. These short, ephemeral videos and images provide a dynamic and engaging way to connect with your audience. Your designs for Instagram Stories should be even more visually dynamic, often incorporating animations, text overlays, and interactive elements such as polls and quizzes. Canva's templates and animation tools make it easy to create captivating Stories that stand out in a user's feed. Think about using a series of images or videos to tell a coherent story, guiding users through a narrative. This sequential approach ensures that users are engaged throughout the experience, boosting your brand's visibility and recall.

Moving on to Facebook, we encounter a platform with a more diverse user base and a wider range of content formats. Facebook supports a variety of image and video sizes, so it's essential to choose the appropriate dimensions for your design. Unlike Instagram, where visually striking graphics reign supreme, Facebook posts benefit from a balance between visual appeal and informative content. Clear and concise text remains a critical component of successful Facebook posts, guiding users towards understanding the message and prompting engagement. Facebook also favors less heavily saturated colors and images compared to Instagram, opting for cleaner and less flashy aesthetics.

Think about incorporating clear calls to action (CTAs) in your Facebook designs. This could be a link to your website, a prompt to like your page, or an invitation to participate in a comment thread. Such CTAs are vital in driving user engagement, leading to enhanced visibility and amplified brand awareness. A well-placed and clearly visible CTA can significantly increase your post's effectiveness. Consider using a striking color or a visually distinct button to emphasize the CTA and guide users to take the desired action.

Facebook also supports different content formats, including live videos and carousels. Live videos provide an opportunity for real-time interaction with your audience, while carousels allow users to swipe through a series of images, extending engagement. Canva can be used to create visually appealing assets for these formats, maximizing their potential to build audience engagement. When creating Facebook carousels, remember that each image should contribute to the overall narrative, creating a cohesive and engaging storytelling experience. Consistent branding and a logical flow between slides are crucial for successful carousel posts.

Twitter, known for its brevity, requires concise and impactful designs. Twitter's character limits influence your text choices; keep your captions short and to the point. The visual element should complement this brevity, focusing on easily digestible images or videos. Twitter's image size requirements are relatively small, so optimize your designs for quick loading times and compatibility with various screen sizes. Consider using strong visuals that convey your message effectively, even within the space constraints imposed by the platform.

Twitter often prioritizes fast-loading, visually arresting images or short videos. Avoid large file sizes to prevent long loading times that can lead to frustration and disengagement. Experiment with high-contrast images and simple layouts to capture user attention quickly, and remember that many Twitter users view content on their mobile devices. Consequently, mobile optimization is vital for achieving optimal display and engagement across various devices.

Finally, let's consider LinkedIn, a platform geared towards professional networking and business development. Unlike the visually driven nature of platforms like Instagram, LinkedIn designs often prioritize professionalism and credibility. This calls for clean and sophisticated designs, usually employing muted colors and professional-looking typography. Avoid overly flashy or casual aesthetics; instead, strive for a polished and refined look that resonates with a professional audience.

Consider using high-quality images of people in professional settings, as these often resonate well with a LinkedIn audience. LinkedIn emphasizes data-driven insights and professional accomplishments; consider incorporating relevant statistics or graphs to demonstrate the value of your content and establish credibility. Remember that your LinkedIn audience is seeking information and professional engagement; ensure that your visuals align with this expectation, avoiding overly casual or playful elements that may appear incongruent with the platform's tone and purpose.

In summary, designing social media graphics effectively necessitates understanding the nuances of each platform.

Each platform has unique visual expectations, preferred content formats, and technical specifications that can significantly influence the impact of your designs. By leveraging Canva's tools and adhering to the best practices outlined for each platform, you can create engaging visuals that drive user engagement and enhance your marketing efforts. Remember to always prioritize clarity, consistency, and platform-specific optimization to achieve the best possible results. Continuously analyze your results, track engagement metrics, and adjust your strategy accordingly to maximize the ROI of your social media design efforts. The evolving nature of these platforms necessitates continuous adaptation and experimentation, ensuring that your designs remain relevant and engaging.

Creating Marketing Materials Flyers and Brochures

Creating effective marketing materials like flyers and brochures requires a strategic approach to design. While Canva simplifies the process, understanding core design principles remains crucial for creating visually appealing and impactful pieces that resonate with your target audience. This section will guide you through the process, emphasizing the importance of layout, visual elements, typography, and color palettes, all within the user-friendly Canva environment.

Let's start with the fundamental element of layout. The layout dictates the arrangement of text and visuals on your flyer or brochure, influencing readability and overall aesthetic appeal. Canva offers a wide range of pre-designed templates to get you started, but understanding the principles behind effective layout is key to customizing these templates or creating your own from scratch. Consider the rule of thirds, a classic design principle that suggests dividing your design into thirds both horizontally and vertically. Placing key elements along these lines creates a more visually balanced and engaging composition. Avoid overcrowding the design; give ample white space (or negative space) to allow elements to breathe and prevent a cluttered look. White space isn't just empty space; it's a design element that helps to guide the reader's eye and improve readability.

The visual hierarchy of your design is also critical. What do you want the reader to see first? The most important information—whether it's a headline, a striking image, or a compelling call to action—should be the focal point, visually emphasized through size, color, or placement. Subsequent elements should be arranged in decreasing order of importance, guiding the reader's eye naturally through the information. Think about using visual cues like size, contrast, and proximity to create this hierarchy. Larger images or text will naturally draw more attention than smaller ones. Elements placed closer together visually group them, implying a connection.

Next, let's delve into choosing appropriate visuals. Images and graphics are essential for capturing attention and communicating your message effectively. Canva offers access to a vast library of stock photos and illustrations, but you should always choose images that are relevant to your message and high-resolution enough to look sharp and professional when printed or viewed online. Blurry or pixelated images can significantly detract from the overall quality of your design. If you have your own high-quality images, incorporating them will further personalize your marketing materials, building brand consistency.

Beyond stock imagery, consider incorporating other visual elements. Icons can be particularly effective for quickly conveying information, often more so than large blocks of text. Canva's icon library offers a wealth of options, allowing you to choose icons that complement your design and reinforce your message. Infographics, when appropriate, can be a powerful tool for presenting data in a visually engaging format, making complex information more easily digestible. Remember to maintain visual consistency throughout your design; ensure that all images, icons, and graphics work together to create a cohesive and professional look.

Typography plays a crucial role in readability and overall design aesthetics. Canva offers a vast selection of fonts, but choosing the right fonts is crucial for conveying your brand's personality and ensuring readability. Avoid using too many different fonts; stick to a maximum of two or three to maintain visual consistency. Generally, it's best to pair one serif font (with small decorative strokes at the end of letters) with one sans-serif font (without strokes) for a balanced look. Serif fonts are often preferred for body text, as their strokes can improve readability, whereas sans-serif fonts tend to work better for headings and other shorter text elements due to their clean, modern look. Consider the readability of your chosen fonts; choose font sizes and styles that are easily readable, especially at smaller sizes on printed materials. Ensure there's sufficient contrast between the text and the background color for optimal legibility.

Color plays a pivotal role in setting the mood and conveying your brand's personality. The colors you choose should align with your brand's identity and target audience. Canva's color tools allow you to select colors from a palette or input hex codes for precise control. Using a color palette generator can assist you in creating a cohesive color scheme. However, remember that color psychology plays a significant role. Certain colors evoke specific emotions and associations. For example, blues often convey trust and calmness, while reds tend to evoke excitement and energy. Understand how different colors can impact your audience's perception of your brand and tailor your choices accordingly. Consider creating a color palette based on your brand's existing colors or creating a new one that aligns with your specific marketing objectives.

Creating a flyer for an upcoming event involves carefully balancing visual appeal with essential information. Prioritize key information like the event date, time, location, and a brief description. Use a compelling headline to grab attention immediately, followed by supporting information presented in a clear and concise manner. Incorporate high-quality images or graphics to enhance the visual appeal, reflecting the event's theme or atmosphere. Consider using a call to action—a clear instruction for the reader to take the next step, such as visiting a website or purchasing tickets. The layout should be clean and uncluttered, guiding the reader's eye seamlessly through the key information.

Designing a brochure for a product or service requires a more detailed approach. Brochures often provide more in-depth information than flyers, so clear organization is essential. Use headings and subheadings to break up the text into digestible chunks. Incorporate high-quality images or graphics showcasing the product or service's features and benefits. The layout can use a tri-fold or bifold design, enabling a clear flow of information. Each section should have a specific purpose—for example, an introduction, a detailed description, testimonials, and contact information. The design should be visually appealing but also informative, building credibility and trust in your brand. A well-designed brochure can serve as a valuable marketing tool, leaving a lasting impression on potential customers.

Remember to always review your work critically, paying close attention to details such as font sizes, image quality, and color consistency. Print a test copy of your flyer or brochure (if applicable) to check the final output's appearance and ensure everything is as expected. Seek feedback from others; a fresh perspective can often highlight areas for improvement. The process of designing marketing materials is iterative; don't hesitate to refine and adjust your design until you're fully satisfied with the final product. By mastering these principles and leveraging Canva's capabilities, you can create marketing materials that effectively communicate your message, capture attention, and ultimately, achieve your marketing goals. The key is to combine Canva's ease of use with a solid understanding of design principles, resulting in professional and visually compelling marketing materials.

Designing Presentations and Infographics

Designing presentations and infographics requires a different approach than creating static marketing materials like flyers and brochures. While the underlying design principles remain the same—considerations of layout, visual hierarchy, typography, and color—the dynamic nature of presentations and the data-centric nature of infographics necessitate a slightly altered strategy. Canva, with its intuitive interface and vast resource library, provides the perfect toolset to master these specialized design projects.

Let's begin with presentations. The effectiveness of a presentation hinges on its ability to clearly and concisely convey information, capturing and holding the audience's attention. Structure is paramount. Before even opening Canva, plan your presentation's content meticulously. Outline the key points, develop a logical flow, and determine the type of visual aids needed to support each point. Will you use images, charts, graphs, or a combination thereof? The narrative should unfold naturally, guiding the viewer through your message with clarity and purpose. Avoid overwhelming your audience with too much text on each slide; instead, focus on delivering key information concisely, using visuals to complement and enhance your message.

Canva's templates provide excellent starting points for presentations. They offer a variety of pre-designed layouts tailored to different presentation styles and purposes. However, don't be afraid to customize these templates to reflect your unique brand identity and the specific message you wish to convey. Think about your audience. A presentation for a business meeting will require a different approach than a presentation for an educational seminar.

Consider the tone you wish to set: formal, informal, professional, or playful. Your design choices should reflect this tone.

Visual hierarchy remains critical in presentation design. What is the most crucial piece of information you want your audience to retain? Emphasize this information through size, color, and placement. Use larger fonts for headlines and key takeaways, and employ contrasting colors to draw attention to important elements. White space, as with other design projects, remains an essential component. Avoid overcrowding slides; allow elements to breathe, ensuring readability and visual comfort for your audience. A visually cluttered slide will distract from your message and impede your ability to effectively communicate your key points.

Typography in presentations requires careful consideration. As before, stick to a limited number of fonts – two or three at most – to maintain visual consistency. Consider using a sans-serif font for headlines and a serif font for body text, ensuring good readability across all text sizes. Varying font sizes to establish a visual hierarchy aids in guiding the viewer's eye through the information presented on each slide. Ensure ample contrast between text color and background color, maintaining optimal legibility, especially in large auditorium settings where projected presentations might be viewed from a distance.

Images and graphics should complement your text, never compete with it. Use high-resolution visuals that are relevant to your content and aesthetically pleasing. Canva's image library offers a vast selection of stock photos and illustrations, but always strive to select images that reflect a professional quality and resonate with your presentation's overall tone. Avoid low-resolution images; they detract from the presentation's overall professionalism. If relevant, consider incorporating charts and graphs to present data clearly and efficiently. Canva provides excellent tools for creating various charts, including bar charts, line graphs, pie charts, and more. Ensure that charts and graphs are labeled clearly and easily understood, and maintain visual consistency with the overall presentation design.

Animations and transitions, used judiciously, can greatly enhance the dynamic nature of a presentation. Canva offers a variety of animation and transition effects that can subtly emphasize key points or add a touch of visual interest. However, avoid overusing these effects; excessive animation can be distracting and detract from your message. Subtle animations can subtly guide your audience's eye, making your presentation more engaging and memorable. The key is to use animation to enhance your presentation's flow and emphasize important information. Don't let animations overtake the message itself.

Next, let's address infographics. Infographics are essentially visual representations of data or information. Their goal is to present complex information in a clear, concise, and visually engaging manner. Effective infographics require a keen understanding of data visualization principles and a thoughtful approach to design. Before even beginning to design an infographic in Canva, plan the data you want to present and the story you wish to tell. Determine the best visual representation for your data – bar charts, pie charts, line graphs, maps, or icons? – and choose representations that best suit the data being conveyed. A clear narrative arc, akin to a story structure, is key to the efficacy of your infographic.

Canva's pre-designed infographic templates offer a solid foundation. However, remember that customization is crucial to effectively communicate your specific information.

Choose a template that aligns with the style and tone of your message. Use color strategically to emphasize key data points and create visual interest. As with presentations, maintain a consistent color palette to maintain visual coherence. The consistent use of color throughout your infographic will help reinforce your message and make it more easily understood by your audience.

Typography in infographics, as in all design projects, plays a critical role in readability. Ensure that all text is clear, concise, and easily readable. Use a variety of font sizes and weights to create a visual hierarchy, guiding the viewer's eye through the information presented. Select fonts that are both aesthetically pleasing and highly legible, even at smaller sizes. The visual hierarchy of your infographic should emphasize the most important data points, leading your audience through your information.

Icons and other visual elements are extremely useful tools in infographics. Canva's vast library of icons provides a wealth of options for illustrating data points or concepts. Select icons that are visually appealing and relevant to the information being presented. Consistent visual elements will enhance the understanding and memorability of your infographic, aiding your audience's comprehension.

When creating infographics, aim for simplicity and clarity. Avoid overcrowding the design with too much information or visual elements. A cluttered infographic is difficult to understand and will ultimately fail to effectively convey your message. Instead, focus on highlighting the most important data points and using visuals to support your narrative. Remember, the goal of an infographic is to simplify complex information, not make it more confusing. Ensure that your infographic is easy to read and understand at a glance. This will ensure that your audience will grasp the key points with ease.

Finally, review your work critically. Examine your presentations and infographics for any inconsistencies or areas for improvement. Pay close attention to detail, ensuring that all text and visuals are clear, concise, and easy to understand. Seek feedback from others, as a fresh perspective can often highlight areas that may have been missed. The iterative process of design refinement is crucial for creating impactful visuals. By applying these principles and leveraging Canva's capabilities, you can create dynamic presentations and informative infographics that effectively communicate your message and leave a lasting impression on your audience. Remember, clear communication is paramount, and a well-designed visual can make all the difference.

Creating Logos and Branding Elements

Creating effective logos and branding elements is crucial for establishing a strong visual identity for any business or organization. This process, while seemingly straightforward, requires careful consideration of design principles and a clear understanding of the brand's message and target audience. Canva, with its intuitive interface and vast resource library, provides an excellent platform for creating professional-looking logos and branding materials, even for those without extensive design experience.

The first step in logo design is brainstorming. Before even opening Canva, dedicate time to thoroughly understand the brand. What are its core values? What message does it aim to convey? Who is its target audience? Answering these questions will help guide your design choices. Consider sketching several initial concepts on paper; this allows for freeform exploration without the constraints of a digital interface. Don't be afraid to experiment with different shapes, symbols, and typography. This initial brainstorming phase is crucial for generating a diverse range of ideas, allowing you to refine and develop your concepts further.

Once you have a few initial sketches, it's time to translate them into digital form using Canva. Canva's intuitive drag-and-drop interface makes this process remarkably user-friendly. Begin by selecting a suitable canvas size; the final dimensions of your logo will depend on its intended uses (website, social media, print materials, etc.). Canva offers various templates, but for logo design, starting with a blank canvas often provides more flexibility.

Color plays a pivotal role in logo design. Your color choices should reflect the brand's personality and evoke specific emotions or associations. For example, a technology company might opt for blues and greys to convey innovation and trustworthiness, while a children's brand might use brighter, more playful colors like yellows and greens. Canva's color palette tool provides a helpful guide, allowing you to experiment with different color combinations and ensure sufficient contrast for readability. Remember the importance of color psychology; research and select colors that resonate with your target audience and effectively communicate the brand's essence. Limit your palette to two or three main colors for visual consistency and cohesiveness. A well-chosen color palette is a crucial element of brand recognition.

Typography is equally crucial. The font you choose should reflect the brand's personality, complementing the overall visual style. A serif font might suggest tradition and elegance, while a sans-serif font could convey modernity and simplicity. As with color, limit yourself to one or two fonts at most to avoid visual clutter and maintain consistency. Ensure the chosen font is legible at various sizes, particularly if the logo will be used in different contexts (e.g., small icons on a website versus large signage). Canva's font library offers a vast selection; experiment with different options until you find the perfect fit for your brand. The readability of your logo is paramount; prioritize clarity and easily distinguishable text.

Simplicity is key in logo design. A successful logo is memorable and easily recognizable, even at small sizes. Avoid overly complex designs or excessive detail, as these can detract from its overall effectiveness. Strive for a clean, uncluttered design that effectively communicates the brand's essence without overwhelming the viewer. A strong logo often achieves more with less; a minimalist approach can often be more impactful. Consider the negative space around your design elements; effective use of negative space can greatly enhance the visual appeal and memorability of your logo.

Once you've finalized your logo design in Canva, consider creating various versions for different applications. You'll likely need a high-resolution version for print materials and a smaller, optimized version for online use. Canva makes it easy to download your design in various formats (JPEG, PNG, SVG) and sizes, ensuring its versatility across different platforms.

Beyond the logo itself, consistent branding extends to other elements like color palettes, fonts, and imagery used across all marketing materials and platforms. This consistency reinforces brand recognition and strengthens the overall brand identity. Canva allows you to create brand kits, which store your chosen colors, fonts, and logos in one centralized location, ensuring consistent application across all your design projects. Using these brand kits makes it effortless to maintain consistent brand identity throughout all your marketing materials.

Let's illustrate this process with a few examples. Imagine designing a logo for a new coffee shop named "The Daily Grind." The brainstorming phase might yield concepts involving coffee beans, coffee cups, or abstract shapes representing the essence of coffee. You might choose warm, earthy tones (browns, creams, oranges) to reflect the warmth and comfort associated with coffee. A simple, elegant serif font might complement the brand's image of traditional craftsmanship. The final logo might feature a stylized coffee bean with the name "The Daily Grind" written beneath it, all in the chosen color palette and font.

Consider another example, a logo for a fitness company called "Peak Performance." Here, you might opt for strong, vibrant colors (blues, greens, perhaps a bold accent color like orange) to suggest energy and motivation. A modern sans-serif font might better align with the brand's forward-thinking approach. The logo might incorporate an upward-pointing arrow or a mountain peak to symbolize the concept of achieving peak performance.

For a tech startup named "InnovateTech," a more minimalist approach might be appropriate. A clean, simple logo featuring a stylized circuit board or a single abstract shape in cool, technological colors (blues, greys, silvers) could communicate innovation and technology effectively. A modern sans-serif font would further reinforce the brand's technologically advanced image.

Creating consistent branding involves applying the same color palette, fonts, and imagery across all marketing materials, from website banners and social media posts to business cards and brochures. Canva simplifies this task with its brand kit feature. By maintaining a cohesive visual identity across all platforms, your brand establishes a recognizable and memorable presence, reinforcing brand loyalty and customer recognition. This consistency builds trust and establishes credibility in the eyes of consumers. Remember that consistent brand identity is essential for achieving long-term brand recognition and building a strong market position. This consistent approach helps customers quickly associate your logo and brand with a particular feeling or experience.

In conclusion, creating logos and branding elements using Canva is a relatively straightforward process, but requires thoughtful planning and a keen understanding of design principles. By carefully considering your brand's identity, target audience, and the message you want to convey, you can create a professional and effective visual identity that resonates with your audience and establishes a strong brand presence. Remember that simplicity, memorability, and consistency are key to successful logo design and overall branding. Use Canva's resources effectively, and experiment with different design options to achieve the best result for your unique brand. The process is iterative; refining your designs based on feedback and testing will ultimately lead to a more impactful and memorable brand image.

Designing Websites and Banners using Canva

Designing effective websites and banners is crucial for online presence. A well-designed banner can capture attention, convey your message, and drive engagement, while a well-structured website mockup allows for planning and visualization before actual development. Canva, with its user-friendly interface and extensive library of templates and resources, offers a streamlined approach to creating these essential web elements, even for those without formal design training.

Before diving into Canva, however, it's essential to define your objectives. What is the purpose of your website banner or website mockup? What message do you want to convey? Who is your target audience? Understanding these key aspects will guide your design decisions and ensure the final product is effective in achieving its intended purpose. Consider the overall tone and style of your brand; your design should align with this established identity, maintaining consistency across all your marketing materials. A cohesive visual identity is key to building brand recognition and trust.

Let's begin with website banners. The first step is determining the appropriate dimensions. Banner sizes vary depending on the platform (social media, email marketing, website header, etc.). Canva provides pre-set dimensions for common banner sizes, making this process simple and efficient. Choosing the correct dimensions ensures your banner displays correctly and avoids distortion or cropping. Researching the specific requirements of the platform where your banner will be used is essential to avoid compatibility issues.

Next, consider the color palette. The colors you choose should reflect your brand's personality and evoke the desired emotions or associations. If your brand is known for its innovative approach, consider a vibrant and energetic color scheme. A more traditional brand might benefit from using more muted and sophisticated colors. Canva's color palette tool facilitates exploration of various color combinations, ensuring sufficient contrast for optimal readability. Remember to limit your palette to a few key colors to maintain visual consistency and cohesiveness; avoid overwhelming the viewer with too much color variation.

Typography plays a crucial role in the effectiveness of your banner. The font you select should be legible, easily readable, and reflect your brand's personality. Choose a font that complements your color palette and overall design aesthetic. Avoid using too many different fonts; two or three, at most, is sufficient to avoid visual clutter and maintain consistency. Prioritize readability; even the most visually appealing font is ineffective if it's difficult to read. Canva's extensive font library provides a wide range of options to choose from.

The placement and hierarchy of text within your banner are also crucial elements. Use a clear and concise message; avoid overwhelming the viewer with too much text. Larger fonts should be reserved for headlines and key phrases, while smaller fonts can be used for supporting text. Properly arranging text is crucial for guiding the viewer's eye and making your message easy to understand at a glance. White space, or negative space, plays a vital role in banner design. It provides visual breathing room and helps to draw attention to key elements.

Imagery is another key aspect of effective banner design. Choose high-quality images that are relevant to your message and visually appealing. Canva offers access to a vast library of stock photos and graphics, simplifying the image selection process. However, ensure that any images used are licensed appropriately and you have the right to use them; avoid copyright infringement. High-quality imagery can greatly enhance the visual appeal and impact of your banner. Ensure your images complement your chosen color palette and overall aesthetic.

Once your banner is complete, download it in the appropriate format (JPEG, PNG) and resolution for the intended platform. Canva allows for easy downloading of designs in various formats and sizes, providing flexibility for different uses. Before publishing, it's important to test the banner on the platform where it will be displayed to ensure it renders correctly.

Let's transition to creating website mockups in Canva. Canva offers a variety of website templates, providing a starting point for your mockup. Select a template that best aligns with your website's purpose and overall design aesthetic. These templates often feature pre-designed sections for different content types (headlines, images, text, calls to action), simplifying the design process.

Using these templates, you can then customize your website's layout and content. Replace placeholder images and text with your own, ensuring consistency with your brand identity. Pay attention to the placement of elements on the page. Good visual hierarchy guides the viewer's eye through the layout in a logical order. Consistent spacing and alignment create a clean, professional look. Balance the visual elements to prevent your mockup from feeling cluttered or overwhelming. Too much text, for example, can make it difficult for viewers to quickly absorb the information. Similarly, too many images can be overwhelming. Finding the right balance is key to effective website design.

Canva's drag-and-drop interface makes it easy to move elements around the page, experiment with different layouts, and refine your design until you are satisfied with the result. Remember to maintain a consistent design style throughout the mockup to create a unified and cohesive website. This consistent visual identity will enhance your website's professional and credible appearance, making a strong first impression on viewers. Remember to consider user experience (UX) in your design. A well-designed website is both visually appealing and easy to navigate.

After creating your mockup, share it with colleagues or clients for feedback. This iterative process of design and revision is essential for refining your design and ensuring it meets your objectives. Canva allows for easy sharing and collaboration, streamlining the feedback process. After incorporating feedback, finalize your mockup and save it for future reference during the actual website development process. This careful planning, using Canva to create mockups, can minimize costly revisions and delays during the website development phase.

Finally, consider creating different versions of your website mockup for different devices (desktop, mobile, tablet). A responsive website design ensures that the site adapts seamlessly to different screen sizes and resolutions. This adaptability is crucial for providing an optimal user experience across all devices. Canva's various template sizes aid in this responsive design.

Creating websites and banners using Canva empowers individuals and businesses to create visually appealing and functional web elements without extensive design experience. By understanding the principles of design and effectively utilizing Canva's features, you can create compelling visuals that communicate your message, engage your audience, and strengthen your online presence. Remember that careful planning, iterative design, and attention to detail are crucial for creating successful web designs. The goal is a visually appealing and intuitive online experience for your users, leading to increased engagement and ultimately, achieving your business objectives.

Understanding and Avoiding LowResolution Images

Understanding and avoiding low-resolution images is paramount in creating professional-looking designs using Canva. Low-resolution images, characterized by pixelation and blurriness, severely detract from the overall quality of your work, no matter how skillfully you've arranged other design elements. This is particularly true when preparing designs for print, where the shortcomings of low-resolution images become drastically amplified. A blurry logo on a business card, for example, immediately undermines the professionalism you're trying to project. In the digital realm, low-resolution images can also affect your brand's credibility, appearing unprofessional on websites, social media, and email marketing campaigns.

The problem with low-resolution images stems from their inherent limitations. Images are composed of pixels, tiny squares of color. High-resolution images have many pixels packed closely together, resulting in a sharp, detailed image. Low-resolution images, conversely, have fewer pixels spread out more thinly. When you enlarge a low-resolution image, the pixels become visible, creating the characteristic blurry or pixelated effect. This is why a small image that looks fine on your screen can appear blurry when printed at a larger size or used in a high-resolution context.

Identifying low-resolution images often requires careful observation. When zooming in on an image in Canva, look for pixelation – those individual squares of color becoming apparent. Blurriness is another clear indicator; the details within the image will appear soft and indistinct. If you suspect an image might be low-resolution, try increasing its size within Canva. If it becomes noticeably blurry or pixelated, it's a strong indication that it lacks sufficient resolution for your intended use.

Finding and utilizing high-resolution images is a crucial step in avoiding these pitfalls. Fortunately, Canva provides a rich library of stock photos, many of which are high-resolution. When searching within Canva, you can often filter by image quality, ensuring that you're only selecting images suitable for print or high-resolution digital applications. Pay close attention to the image details provided; sometimes, the resolution is explicitly stated. If it isn't, you can still visually inspect the image at its largest possible size within Canva before incorporating it into your design.

However, Canva's stock photo library isn't your only source of high-resolution images. You can also upload your own images, provided they are of sufficient resolution. Before uploading, ensure your images are in a suitable format such as JPEG or PNG. Understanding image file formats and their suitability for various purposes is also important. JPEGs are generally preferred for photographic images because of their good balance between file size and image quality, while PNGs are ideal for images with sharp lines, text, or transparent backgrounds. When shooting your own images, using a high-quality camera and shooting at the highest resolution your camera allows is crucial.

Suppose you're working with an image that's already too low-resolution to be enlarged without significant quality loss. In that case, there are techniques for upscaling, although it's important to be aware that this process isn't perfect. Upscaling increases the number of pixels in an image, making it larger. However, it cannot create detail that wasn't originally present. Therefore, significant upscaling of a low-resolution image will always result in some level of blurriness or artifacts (visual imperfections). Canva itself doesn't have built-in sophisticated upscaling features. However, numerous online tools specifically designed for image upscaling can be used. It's advisable to experiment with different upscaling tools to compare results and find the one that produces the best quality. It is often better to start with a higher resolution image to avoid the need for upscaling entirely.

The impact of low-resolution images on print quality is particularly significant. When a design is printed, the image is rendered at a much higher physical resolution than is typically shown on a screen. This means that any flaws in the original image, which may have been barely noticeable on screen, will be dramatically amplified in the print. Pixelation and blurriness will be far more apparent, resulting in a print that looks unprofessional and amateurish. Therefore, always ensure that all your images are of sufficient resolution before sending your designs to a printing service. Confirm the printing company's specifications regarding image resolution; this information is often readily available on their website. Failing to do so could lead to costly reprints or a less than ideal final product.

Ensuring print-ready visuals requires careful consideration of various factors beyond just image resolution. Resolution (measured in DPI or dots per inch) is crucial; generally, 300 DPI is the standard for print-ready images. However, the image itself also needs to be properly prepared. Make sure your color mode is set to CMYK (Cyan, Magenta, Yellow, Key/Black), the standard color model for printing, rather than RGB (Red, Green, Blue) which is predominantly used for screen displays. Converting from RGB to CMYK can slightly alter colors; hence, it's essential to review your design after the conversion to ensure colors still meet your requirements. The file format is also important for print;

PDF is usually the preferred format for print designs as it preserves the design's integrity across different systems and software.

Furthermore, bleeding is another critical element for print-ready visuals. Bleeding refers to extending the design beyond the final trim size of the printed piece. This ensures that there are no white gaps at the edges after trimming. In Canva, most templates already take bleeding into account, but you need to carefully review the design specifications. Adding bleed is crucial for professional-looking prints. You wouldn't want your business card's logo cut off at the edge. Additionally, check your design for sufficient contrast; designs meant for print should have strong contrast between text and background colors to ensure readability and visual clarity.

Using high-resolution images is not just a matter of aesthetic preference; it's a fundamental aspect of professional graphic design. The difference between a design that uses high-quality images and one that doesn't is stark. The former looks sharp, clean, and professional, exuding quality and trustworthiness. The latter looks unprofessional, even amateurish, potentially damaging your brand's reputation. By understanding the importance of resolution, mastering the techniques for finding high-quality images, and implementing the strategies for upscaling images when necessary, you can significantly elevate your Canva designs, making them visually appealing and impactful, regardless of their intended medium. Investing the time to ensure your images meet the necessary resolution requirements will always be worth the effort for the enhanced professionalism and credibility it provides your work. Always prioritize image quality to ensure your designs convey the message and brand identity effectively. The seemingly small detail of image resolution significantly impacts the final result, leaving a lasting impression on your audience.

Correcting Overcrowded Designs and Poor Spacing

Overcrowded designs are a common pitfall in Canva, often stemming from a misunderstanding of visual hierarchy and the crucial role of white space. A visually cluttered design is not only aesthetically unappealing but also significantly impacts readability and the overall effectiveness of your message. Imagine a website banner crammed with text, images, and logos, all vying for attention. The result is a chaotic jumble that confuses rather than informs the viewer. Similarly, a marketing flyer packed with information, leaving little breathing room, loses its impact and potentially repels the reader.

The core problem lies in neglecting the principles of visual hierarchy. Visual hierarchy is the arrangement of elements in a design to guide the viewer's eye and establish a clear order of importance. By strategically prioritizing certain elements, you create a pathway for the viewer's gaze, ensuring that key information is readily noticed while less crucial details recede into the background. Without a deliberate visual hierarchy, all elements compete for attention, leading to a sense of chaos and confusion. A well-structured design, on the other hand, seamlessly guides the viewer through the information, ensuring your message is communicated effectively.

One of the most effective ways to establish a strong visual hierarchy and combat overcrowding is through the judicious use of white space, also known as negative space. White space isn't simply empty space; it's an integral design element that provides visual breathing room, enhancing readability and creating a more balanced and sophisticated aesthetic. It acts as a visual buffer between elements, preventing them from feeling cramped and overwhelming. Think of it as the quiet spaces between musical notes – essential for the melody to unfold gracefully.

The amount of white space needed varies depending on the design and its purpose. A minimalist design might feature generous amounts of white space, showcasing a few carefully chosen elements. Conversely, a more complex design may use less white space, but its distribution should remain strategic and intentional. The key is to strike a balance. Too much white space can lead to a sparse, unengaging design, while too little creates a sense of visual clutter.

Identifying overcrowded designs requires a critical eye. Look for areas where elements feel cramped together. Is the text too densely packed? Are images overlapping or competing for attention? Is there sufficient visual separation between different sections of the design? If you find yourself struggling to focus on a specific element, or if your design feels overwhelming at a glance, chances are it's overcrowded.

Let's consider some practical examples. Suppose you're designing a poster for an event. Instead of cramming all the information – date, time, location, ticket details, contact information – into a single, dense block of text, break it down into smaller, more digestible chunks. Use different font sizes and styles to emphasize key information, such as the date and time, while secondary details can use smaller fonts. Incorporate visual elements, such as icons or images, to enhance visual interest and guide the eye. Leave sufficient white space around each section to allow for visual breathing room.

Another common scenario is a business card overloaded with information. Resist the urge to fit every detail onto the card. Prioritize the most crucial information – your name, title, contact details, and logo. Use a clean, uncluttered layout with ample white space. Overcrowding a business card undermines its professional appearance and makes it difficult for potential clients to quickly and easily grasp your key information.

In Canva, correcting overcrowding often involves simple adjustments. Begin by grouping related elements. This allows you to manipulate them as a single unit, ensuring consistent spacing between different sections. Experiment with different layouts. Try rearranging elements, adding or removing white space, and altering the sizes of images and text boxes. Canva's grid feature can be a valuable tool for creating a balanced and well-organized layout. Use the grid to align elements, ensuring consistent spacing and avoiding visual chaos.

Improving spacing is equally important. Canva provides various tools for controlling spacing, including adjustable margins and padding around text boxes and images. Use these features to create visual breathing room. Experiment with different spacing values until you find a layout that feels balanced and uncluttered. Consistency is key; ensure that spacing is consistent throughout your design to avoid a jarring and disjointed appearance.

Incorporating visual cues such as lines or dividers can also enhance visual hierarchy and improve spacing. Lines can create visual separation between different sections of your design, while dividers can segment content effectively, making it easier to scan and process information. However, use lines and dividers sparingly, as excessive use can lead to an overly busy design. Always strive for a sense of simplicity and elegance.

Don't be afraid to experiment. Create multiple versions of your design, trying different layouts, spacing variations, and font choices. Step back from your design periodically to view it with fresh eyes. Ask yourself: Is the information easy to read? Is the design visually appealing? Does it clearly convey its intended message? If you answer "no" to any of these questions, it's a clear signal that further refinement is needed.

Remember, the goal is to create a design that is both visually appealing and easy to understand. Avoid overcrowding your designs by embracing the power of visual hierarchy and the importance of white space. By mastering these fundamental design principles, you can transform your Canva creations from cluttered messes into clean, professional, and impactful designs. Consistent practice and attention to detail will refine your ability to spot and rectify overcrowded designs, creating visually compelling work that effectively communicates your intended message. The investment of time and effort in creating a well-spaced and uncluttered design will significantly impact the effectiveness and impact of your Canva creations.

Fixing Inconsistent Branding and Typography

Maintaining a consistent brand identity is paramount in today's visually-driven world. Inconsistent branding undermines your credibility and dilutes the impact of your message. Think of a company whose logo changes color from one advertisement to the next, or whose font choices vary wildly across their website, social media, and printed materials. The result is a confusing and unprofessional image that fails to resonate with the audience. Consistent branding, conversely, creates a cohesive and memorable identity, instantly recognizable and easily associated with your brand's values and message. This section will delve into how to achieve that visual harmony, especially within the Canva environment.

One of the primary pillars of consistent branding is maintaining a consistent color palette. Choosing a specific set of colors and adhering to them across all your designs is crucial. This doesn't mean you can't use variations or accents; subtle shifts in saturation or brightness can add visual interest without compromising overall consistency. However, the core colors – your brand colors – should remain constant. Imagine a fashion brand using different shades of red across its website, social media posts, and product packaging. The inconsistency creates a fractured identity, undermining the brand's carefully cultivated aesthetic. By establishing and adhering to a core palette, the brand reinforces its visual identity, making it easily recognizable and memorable.

In Canva, maintaining color consistency is relatively straightforward. Canva's color palette feature allows you to save your chosen colors, ensuring you can easily access and use them across various projects. You can even create "brand kits" within Canva, storing not only your colors but also your chosen fonts and logo, streamlining the design process and ensuring uniformity across all your work. This functionality eliminates guesswork, preventing accidental deviations from your established color scheme. Moreover, Canva allows you to use color codes (HEX, RGB, CMYK) for pinpoint accuracy, guaranteeing that colors are precisely replicated across different platforms and devices. This attention to detail ensures a polished and professional look, bolstering your brand's credibility.

Beyond color, consistent typography plays a crucial role in maintaining a unified brand identity. Choosing a primary font (or a maximum of two for different uses – headings and body text) and sticking with it throughout your designs creates a sense of visual order and professionalism. Imagine a restaurant using a different font for its menu, website, and promotional flyers. This inconsistency can make the restaurant seem disjointed and unprofessional. By consistently employing a well-chosen typeface, the restaurant establishes a visual identity that resonates with its brand, ensuring a harmonious and recognizable experience across all touchpoints.

Canva provides a wide range of fonts, offering a wealth of options to suit various design needs. However, resist the urge to experiment with too many different fonts within a single design, or across multiple designs. This creates visual chaos and detracts from your message. Select fonts that are legible, aesthetically pleasing, and aligned with your brand's personality. For example, a law firm might opt for a sophisticated serif font to convey authority and trustworthiness, while a tech startup might choose a sleek, modern sans-serif font to express innovation and dynamism. The key is to find fonts that resonate with your target audience and complement your brand's overall aesthetic. Canva's font selection tools allow you to easily preview different fonts, ensuring you make informed decisions about typography that align with your brand identity.

Your logo is the cornerstone of your brand identity. It's the visual symbol that represents your company, product, or service. Consistency in logo usage is vital for brand recognition and memorability. It should always be displayed correctly – in the right size, color, and position – across all your design materials. Using an inconsistent logo – different sizes, colors, or even slight variations in its design – creates a fragmented image, diluting its impact and weakening your brand recognition. Imagine a clothing company showcasing its logo in different styles across its website, social media platforms, and product labels. This lack of consistency creates confusion and weakens the overall brand impression. By ensuring consistency in logo presentation, the company strengthens brand recall and reinforces its visual identity.

In Canva, you can easily upload your logo and save it to your brand kit. This ensures you always use the correct version of your logo, preventing inconsistencies. Canva also offers tools to maintain your logo's correct aspect ratio and size, helping you avoid distortion or misrepresentation. This built-in functionality simplifies the process of consistent logo implementation, helping you maintain a unified brand image across all your designs.

Furthermore, consider the context of your designs. While consistency is crucial, sometimes slight adjustments are necessary to adapt your branding to different platforms or mediums. For example, your logo might need to be smaller on a social media post than on a website banner. However, these adjustments should be made thoughtfully, ensuring that the core elements of your branding remain consistent. The logo's color should remain consistent even if its size changes. The primary fonts should be used consistently, even if a secondary font is needed for small captions or annotations. This mindful approach ensures a consistent brand image while accommodating the practical requirements of different design platforms.

Inconsistencies in branding and typography significantly impact a design's overall effectiveness. A design with inconsistent branding lacks cohesion, resulting in a less professional and memorable appearance. This, in turn, can negatively impact how the audience perceives your brand, undermining its credibility and potentially hindering its growth. Conversely, maintaining consistent branding across all your designs reinforces your brand identity, making it more easily recognizable and memorable. Consistent branding builds trust and creates a sense of professionalism, ultimately enhancing the effectiveness of your communication efforts.

Addressing inconsistent branding and typography requires attention to detail and a meticulous approach. The use of brand kits in Canva helps streamline the design process, ensuring consistent use of color palettes, fonts, and logos across all your designs. Regular reviews of your designs are important to catch any inconsistencies before they become larger problems. It's also essential to establish clear guidelines for your brand's visual identity, ensuring that everyone involved in creating designs adheres to those standards. This approach guarantees visual unity across all your marketing materials and digital assets.

Remember, effective design isn't just about aesthetics; it's about conveying a clear message and creating a lasting impression. Consistency in branding and typography is vital for achieving these goals. By mastering the principles of consistent branding and using Canva's helpful features effectively, you can create visually appealing and professional designs that effectively communicate your message and strengthen your brand identity. Consistent effort and attention to detail in this area will significantly enhance the impact of your designs and ultimately contribute to the success of your brand. Through consistent application of these techniques, you can create a powerful and unified brand image that resonates with your audience and helps you achieve your design goals.

Troubleshooting Common Canva Issues

Troubleshooting common Canva issues often involves a blend of technical know-how and understanding Canva's interface. Let's delve into some frequent problems and their solutions, transforming frustration into effortless design.

One of the most common hurdles is uploading files. Canva supports a range of file types, but sometimes uploads fail or images appear distorted. If an image won't upload, ensure it meets Canva's size and file type restrictions. Large files can take longer to upload, so patience is key; however, excessively large files may need to be compressed before uploading. Tools like TinyPNG or Compressor.io can significantly reduce file size without substantial quality loss. Another common culprit is an incorrect file format – Canva primarily uses JPG, PNG, and SVG. If your file is in a less common format (like TIFF or AI), try converting it using a free online converter before attempting to upload it. Sometimes, a corrupted file prevents successful uploads; try re-saving or creating a fresh version of the problematic file. If the issue persists, Canva's help center often provides troubleshooting steps specific to file upload problems, and contacting their support team directly can resolve particularly stubborn issues. Remember to check your internet connection as well; a weak or unstable connection can interrupt the upload process. Finally, ensure that you are using a supported web browser or Canva's app, as older or incompatible versions can lead to unexpected issues.

Formatting problems are another significant source of Canva frustration. These often stem from inconsistent application of design principles or issues with text boxes, images, and elements' placement. Text can unexpectedly jump lines or refuse to wrap properly, especially when using unusual fonts or complex formatting within Canva. Double-check your text box settings; ensure that the text wrapping is appropriately configured and that the font size is compatible with the space allocated. If you're using a custom font, it might not be fully compatible with Canva's rendering engine. Try substituting the font with a standard Canva option to see if this resolves the formatting issue. Poor image resolution leads to blurry or pixelated results after uploading, especially when scaling images larger than their original dimensions. Always use high-resolution images for optimal clarity, and avoid enlarging them excessively within Canva. Consider alternative images with better resolution if enlargement is necessary. Lastly, unintentional changes to element layering can create formatting discrepancies. Canva's layering system allows you to arrange design elements; overlapping elements sometimes obscure each other unpredictably. Utilize Canva's layer panel to check the order of your elements and rearrange them accordingly. Regularly save your progress to avoid the frustration of losing work. The "autosave" function in Canva helps mitigate data loss but creating manual saves at regular intervals adds a crucial layer of safety.

Difficulties with specific Canva features often highlight a lack of understanding or familiarity with their functionality. For instance, the animation feature, a powerful tool for creating engaging visuals, requires careful coordination and awareness of its settings. Improperly set animations can result in jerky or unexpected movements. Start with simpler animations, gradually mastering more advanced options. Canva's help section contains tutorials for many of its functions, offering detailed explanations and practical examples. Exploring these tutorials can greatly increase your proficiency and avoid issues stemming from a lack of knowledge. Another common problem arises with interactive features, such as buttons or links. Incorrectly configured interactive elements can be non-functional or lead to broken links. Carefully review the instructions and settings when adding these features, ensuring that all required information is accurately entered. Always test interactive elements thoroughly after creation to confirm functionality.

Troubleshooting issues with templates within Canva hinges on understanding how templates are structured. Sometimes elements within a template can appear locked or uneditable, preventing customization. This is often due to template restrictions, designed to maintain the original aesthetic. Check the template's settings to see if elements are indeed locked. If so, you may need to duplicate the template to unlock its components for editing. Ensure that you are working on the correct layer or that you have not inadvertently selected a locked layer containing the elements you wish to edit. If you find a template is unusable, contacting Canva support or selecting a different template may be necessary.

Canva's collaborative features, although useful, can sometimes cause issues. Multiple users editing a design simultaneously can lead to conflicts or overwriting, resulting in lost work or unexpected changes. To avoid this, communicate effectively among collaborators, outlining individual roles and responsibilities within the design process. Establish a clear workflow that minimizes the chance of accidental overwrites. Canva's version history feature is invaluable in collaborative projects; it allows users to revert to previous versions if necessary. However, it's crucial to save your work frequently to minimize the impact of accidental data loss during collaboration.

Working offline is another common area of concern. Canva's core functionality is web-based, and offline access is limited. However, some features might allow limited offline editing capabilities within Canva's mobile app; check your app's functionalities to confirm this. If you need to design without a stable internet connection, consider using alternative design software with better offline capabilities or exporting your Canva project as an image for offline viewing.

Dealing with unexpected errors or glitches within Canva is a frustrating experience. Errors can range from simple loading problems to more complex system failures. The first step is to check your internet connection; a slow or unstable connection can lead to various issues. Clearing your browser cache and cookies is also beneficial; outdated information stored in your browser can sometimes interfere with Canva's functionality. If the problem persists, trying a different browser or device can help isolate whether the issue lies within Canva or your specific setup. If the problem is persistent, reaching out to Canva's support team through their help center is advisable. They can provide more specific troubleshooting steps tailored to the specific error you encounter and even provide temporary workarounds while they address the problem. Always document the error you encounter, including screenshots, to aid in the troubleshooting process.

Throughout your Canva journey, remember that seeking help is not a sign of weakness. Canva's extensive help center contains articles and tutorials addressing numerous issues. Their support team is available to assist with more complex problems. Actively utilizing these resources not only saves time and frustration, but also enhances your overall design proficiency within the platform. The key is to be proactive and systematically explore the available troubleshooting resources before succumbing to despair. Through perseverance and resourcefulness, you can overcome most of Canva's challenges, unlocking your creative potential.

Improving Readability and Visual Hierarchy

Improving the readability and visual hierarchy of your Canva designs is crucial for effective communication. A well-structured design guides the viewer's eye effortlessly, ensuring your message is received clearly and efficiently. Poor readability and a muddled visual hierarchy, conversely, can lead to confusion and frustration, leaving your audience struggling to understand your intended message. Let's explore practical strategies to elevate your Canva designs in this respect.

One of the most fundamental aspects of effective design is text readability. This goes beyond simply choosing a font; it encompasses several key elements. Firstly, consider the font itself. Avoid overly decorative or stylized fonts, especially for large blocks of text. These can be difficult to read, especially at smaller sizes. Opt for clean, legible fonts like Open Sans, Lato, or Roboto, which are widely considered to be highly readable. These fonts are designed with clear letterforms and consistent spacing, ensuring effortless reading even in smaller sizes or on various devices. Experiment with different font weights (light, regular, bold) to create visual interest and hierarchy but ensure sufficient contrast between the text and the background to maintain readability.

Next, pay close attention to font size. Text that is too small strains the eyes, rendering it unreadable. Conversely, text that is too large can appear overwhelming and disrupt the overall design balance. Use a hierarchy of font sizes to guide the reader through your content. The most important information should be displayed in larger, bolder fonts, while less critical information can be rendered in smaller sizes.

Consider the context of your design; longer blocks of text require larger font sizes to ensure readability. Shorter captions or headlines can utilize smaller, more decorative fonts without compromising comprehension.

Choosing the right color contrast between your text and background is paramount. Insufficient contrast makes text difficult to read and can cause eye strain. Use a contrast checker tool (many free online tools are available) to ensure that your text color provides sufficient contrast against its background. This is especially crucial for individuals with visual impairments. Aim for a significant contrast ratio, generally above 4.5:1 for optimal readability, especially with longer text segments. When choosing your colour palette, remember to choose colors that not only complement each other but also ensure readability.

Leading, or the space between lines of text, greatly influences readability. Insufficient leading leads to cramped text, making it hard to read and appearing cluttered. Excessive leading, however, can make the text appear sparse and less cohesive. Experiment with different leading values to find what best suits your design and text content. Canva offers easy-to-use options for adjusting line spacing, allowing you to fine-tune the leading to ensure optimal readability for your particular font and text blocks. Consider the overall design; long paragraphs benefit from more leading, whilst short captions or headings may benefit from tighter leading.

Visual hierarchy is the arrangement of elements to guide the viewer's eye through a design. A well-structured visual hierarchy directs the audience's attention to the most important information first. You achieve this through a combination of visual cues, size, color, and placement. Using a clear visual hierarchy ensures that your message is received in the intended sequence.

Size plays a significant role in establishing visual hierarchy. Larger elements naturally draw the eye first. Use this to your advantage by making your most important elements the largest. This could be a headline, a key image, or a call to action button. Make this element significantly larger than other elements to guide the viewer's attention. In a complex layout, this strategy simplifies viewer navigation.

Color is another powerful tool for creating visual hierarchy. Using a color scheme with strong contrasting colors helps to emphasize certain elements. Bright, saturated colors attract the eye more than muted tones. Use bright colors strategically to highlight crucial elements, while utilizing more subdued colors for less important information, such as background elements. Think about the psychology of color – some colors inspire action, while others evoke calmness; strategically use this to your advantage.

Placement also influences visual hierarchy. Elements placed centrally or in prominent positions are noticed first. Strategic placement complements size and color in emphasizing significant aspects of your design. For instance, a large headline placed at the top of a page immediately captures the viewer's attention.

White space, or negative space, is often overlooked but is crucial in establishing visual hierarchy. Adequate white space separates elements, preventing visual clutter and making your design look clean and professional. It allows the eye to rest and focuses attention on individual components. Consider the overall flow; white space can direct the eye along a specific path through your design.

Effective use of white space can dramatically increase the overall clarity and impact of your design.

Use visual cues to guide the eye. Arrows, lines, and other graphic elements can be used to direct attention to specific areas. These subtle yet impactful elements can highlight particular details or key information. Experiment with different styles of arrows or lines to complement the rest of your design. Remember to choose visual cues that are aesthetically pleasing while ensuring they don't disrupt the overall design.

Combining these techniques is crucial. Consider the relationship between size, color, placement, white space, and visual cues. A successful visual hierarchy uses all these elements in harmony, working together to guide the viewer's eye naturally through your design. Remember to always keep in mind the purpose of your design. Prioritize elements that support your message effectively.

Consistency is key. Maintain a consistent visual style throughout your design. This includes consistent use of fonts, colors, and spacing. Inconsistency can confuse the viewer and weaken the impact of your design. Ensure that all elements work together in a harmonious way. Think of your design as a story; guide your viewer through it coherently.

Finally, remember to test your designs. After you have created your design, take some time to review it from a viewer's perspective. Is the information easily accessible? Does the visual hierarchy guide the eye appropriately? Is the overall message clear? Testing allows you to assess the efficacy of your design, which is essential in ensuring successful communication. Seek feedback from others; a fresh perspective can identify areas for improvement that you may have overlooked.

By carefully considering text readability and implementing a clear visual hierarchy, you significantly enhance the impact and effectiveness of your Canva designs. These seemingly simple techniques, when applied effectively, transform your designs from cluttered and confusing to clear and compelling. Mastering these principles empowers you to create professional-quality designs that effectively communicate your message to your audience.

Utilizing Canvas Pro Features

Canva Pro unlocks a suite of powerful features designed to streamline your workflow and elevate the quality of your designs. While the free version offers a solid foundation for creating visuals, the Pro version introduces significant enhancements that justify its cost for many users, particularly those who create designs frequently or require advanced functionalities. Let's delve into the key features that distinguish Canva Pro and explore how they can transform your design process.

One of the most valuable features of Canva Pro is the Brand Kit. This tool allows you to meticulously define your brand's visual identity, ensuring consistency across all your designs. You can upload your logos, specify your brand colors (with precise hex codes), and select your preferred fonts. This eliminates the need to repeatedly input these elements manually for each project, saving significant time and reducing the risk of inconsistencies. Imagine designing a series of social media posts or marketing materials – the Brand Kit ensures that every element, from the logo placement to the font choices, flawlessly reflects your brand's aesthetic. This level of consistency is invaluable for maintaining a professional image and building brand recognition. The free version allows for limited color palette management, but the Pro version's comprehensive control over brand assets offers an unmatched level of precision and efficiency. The time saved by automatically applying your brand's consistent visual identity across multiple projects adds up significantly, making it a worthwhile investment for businesses and individuals with established branding.

Beyond brand consistency, Canva Pro introduces "Magic Resize," a game-changer for adapting designs across multiple platforms. Need to transform a Facebook post into an Instagram story, a Twitter header into a LinkedIn banner, or a Pinterest image into a YouTube thumbnail? With Magic Resize, you can effortlessly adjust your designs to fit various dimensions without compromising visual quality. This feature drastically reduces the time spent recreating designs for different platforms. Instead of starting from scratch each time, you can quickly resize your existing design, making minor adjustments as needed. Consider the scenario of preparing a marketing campaign across multiple social media channels; the free version would require painstaking manual resizing, while the Pro version allows you to effortlessly repurpose one master design, saving immense time and effort. This not only saves time but also ensures visual consistency across your entire marketing campaign, creating a more cohesive and professional brand presence. The ease and speed of Magic Resize make it a key selling point for Canva Pro, especially for those involved in content marketing or social media management.

Content planning and scheduling become much more efficient with Canva Pro's integration with various scheduling tools. This feature is particularly beneficial for social media managers and content creators who need to plan and schedule their posts in advance. The seamless connection between Canva and these scheduling platforms allows for a streamlined workflow, eliminating the need to switch between multiple applications. The time saved by managing your entire content creation and scheduling process within Canva's ecosystem translates to increased efficiency and productivity. This feature isn't solely about convenience; it reduces the risk of errors and inconsistencies that can arise from managing design and scheduling across disparate platforms. The integrated scheduling feature simplifies the workflow, allowing for a more focused approach to content creation and strategic posting.

Canva Pro also offers a significantly expanded library of templates, stock photos, videos, and illustrations. While the free version offers a reasonable selection, the Pro version provides access to a much larger and more diverse collection of high-quality resources. This expanded library allows for greater creativity and design flexibility. When designing, the availability of diverse and high-quality resources is crucial for creating visually compelling content. The wider range of options available in Canva Pro can drastically reduce the time spent searching for suitable elements, and the higher quality of the assets available contributes to a more professional final product. The cost savings from not needing to purchase stock photos or illustrations elsewhere can, over time, offset the cost of the Pro subscription.

Another significant advantage of Canva Pro lies in the enhanced collaboration features. The ability to share designs with others and work collaboratively on projects in real-time streamlines team projects, allowing for a smoother workflow and faster design cycles. This feature is indispensable for teams working on design projects together, fostering improved communication and efficiency. Real-time collaboration ensures everyone is on the same page, reducing confusion and avoiding unnecessary back-and-forth communication. The ability to easily share and edit designs allows for rapid iteration and feedback, accelerating the design process.

The increased storage capacity offered by Canva Pro is particularly valuable for those who work with many large-resolution images and videos. The free version's storage limitations can often hinder creativity and efficiency. The larger storage provided in Canva Pro eliminates these constraints, providing the freedom to work with large files and a larger number of assets without worrying about storage limitations. This is a crucial factor for designers who work with high-resolution images and videos, as it allows them to maintain a streamlined workflow without the constant concern about exceeding storage limits. This unrestricted storage capacity becomes increasingly valuable as your design portfolio expands.

Beyond the individual features, the overall user experience of Canva Pro is noticeably smoother. The free version, while functional, can sometimes experience minor performance issues. Canva Pro offers a consistently faster and more responsive design experience, enabling a more fluid and efficient creative workflow. The enhanced performance minimizes downtime and interruptions during the design process, allowing you to maintain a consistent focus on your work. This subtle but significant improvement in performance is crucial for maintaining productivity and preventing disruptions to the creative process.

Finally, let's consider a cost-benefit analysis. While the Canva Pro subscription involves a monthly or annual fee, the return on investment can be substantial. The time saved through features like Magic Resize and the Brand Kit, the enhanced quality of designs due to access to a larger library of resources, and the increased efficiency of collaboration tools all contribute to a significant productivity boost. For individuals or businesses that use Canva regularly for professional designs, the cost savings in time and resources frequently outweigh the subscription cost. The improved design quality resulting from the Pro features can lead to better outcomes in marketing, branding, and communication, further justifying the investment.

In conclusion, Canva Pro offers a comprehensive range of advanced features that significantly improve the design process. While the free version is excellent for basic design needs, the Pro version elevates the experience to a professional level, offering unparalleled efficiency, enhanced quality, and seamless collaboration capabilities. The cost-benefit analysis strongly suggests that for frequent users or those seeking professional-level results, the investment in Canva Pro offers a significant return in terms of time, efficiency, and design quality. The key is to evaluate your specific needs and design workflow to determine whether the enhanced features justify the upgrade to Canva Pro.

Creating Animations and GIFs in Canva

Canva's animation features, readily accessible even in the free version, offer a powerful way to breathe life into your designs. Transforming static images into engaging, moving visuals can significantly increase their impact and memorability. While Canva doesn't offer the sophisticated keyframe animation found in professional animation software, its built-in tools are surprisingly versatile for creating simple, effective animations and GIFs perfectly suited for social media, presentations, and even short marketing videos.

Let's begin with the fundamental process. Creating animations in Canva typically involves using the "Animate" feature found within the editor. Once you've designed your base image or series of images within Canva, select the element you want to animate – this could be a single image, a text box, or even a group of elements. After selecting, click on the "Animate" button located in the editor's toolbar. You'll find a variety of animation styles to choose from, categorized broadly into "Entrance," "Emphasis," and "Exit" animations.

Entrance animations bring elements onto the screen; think of a fade-in, a zoom, or a slide from a specific direction. Emphasis animations draw attention to existing elements, perhaps with a bounce, a shake, or a pulsating effect. Exit animations gracefully remove elements from the screen, mirroring the entrance animations. Experimentation is key here. Try out different animations to see how they affect the overall feel of your design. Observe how different animation speeds impact the visual flow. A fast animation might convey energy and excitement, whereas a slow, deliberate animation might create a sense of calmness or sophistication.

The power of these simple animations lies in their ability to guide the viewer's eye through your design. Consider a presentation slide with multiple key points. Instead of all points appearing simultaneously, you could animate each point to appear sequentially, drawing attention to one idea at a time and enhancing comprehension. This controlled unveiling of information creates a more engaging experience than simply presenting all the information at once. Similarly, in social media posts, subtle animations can draw attention to a call to action, like a button or a specific piece of text, making it stand out and encouraging interaction.

Creating GIFs is a natural extension of Canva's animation capabilities. A GIF is essentially a short, looping animation. In Canva, you can easily create GIFs by animating your design and then downloading it as a GIF file. The platform seamlessly handles the conversion, taking away the complexities of using dedicated GIF-making software. This simplicity makes GIF creation accessible even to those with no prior experience in animation. To generate a GIF, design your animation using the steps described earlier. Once satisfied, click on the download button and select the GIF format. Canva will automatically optimize the GIF for size and quality, ensuring your animation is readily shareable across various platforms without significant file size issues.

Let's illustrate this with concrete examples. Imagine you're designing a promotional graphic for a new product launch. You could create a simple animation where the product image fades in, accompanied by a text box revealing the product name and a brief tagline. This dynamic introduction is far more engaging than a static image. For a social media post announcing a sale, you might animate a price tag "falling" or "disappearing" to visually represent the discount. A simple shake animation can highlight a key feature of your product, or a subtle zoom can bring focus to an important piece of text. The possibilities are extensive and depend solely on your creativity.

Beyond single-element animations, Canva allows you to animate multiple elements in sequence or simultaneously. This opens up exciting avenues for more complex animations. Consider animating a sequence of images to create a short slideshow-style GIF for a product demonstration or a quick story recap. This might involve animating images one after another, with a slight delay between each, creating a sense of progression. You could also animate multiple text boxes appearing in succession, revealing key information piece by piece. This technique is effective in creating a sense of anticipation and controlled information delivery.

Optimizing animations for different platforms is crucial. While Canva handles the basic GIF conversion, consider these factors. Platforms like Twitter and Instagram have different optimal GIF dimensions and file size limits. Before downloading, check the platform's specifications and adjust your animation's dimensions accordingly. If your GIF exceeds the recommended file size, try reducing the animation's length or the number of frames to optimize it for faster loading times and better user experience. Remember, a smaller file size leads to quicker loading, enhancing the user experience, especially on mobile devices. A long, large GIF can frustrate users, leading to them skipping past your content.

Furthermore, consider the visual style and context of your intended platform. An animation that works beautifully on Pinterest might not be suitable for LinkedIn. Align your animation style with the general aesthetic and user expectations of your target platform for maximal impact. Avoid overly complex animations on platforms where quick attention spans are the norm, such as Instagram and Twitter. Focus on subtle, impactful animations that complement the overall design rather than overwhelming the user.

Another crucial aspect is ensuring accessibility. Avoid using animations that are distracting or cause discomfort for users with certain sensitivities. If you're using flashing lights or rapid movements, be mindful of potential issues with photosensitive epilepsy. Maintain a balance between visual interest and user comfort. Simple, clean animations are generally preferred for accessibility and broader user appeal.

Let's delve into some advanced techniques. While Canva doesn't offer frame-by-frame animation, you can achieve a similar effect by using multiple pages within a Canva design. Create each frame as a separate page, and then export them individually as images. You can then use external GIF-making software to stitch these images together to form your animation. This method allows for more precise control and allows for animations that are beyond the capabilities of Canva's built-in animation tools. However, this requires extra steps and the utilization of external software.

Understanding color palettes and their impact on animation is paramount. Color can significantly alter the mood and message conveyed. A vibrant color scheme can express enthusiasm and excitement, while muted colors can convey a sense of sophistication or calmness. Consider how your color choices interact with the animation's movements to further enhance the visual narrative. Consistent color usage throughout the animation ensures visual harmony and enhances the overall impact.

Mastering typography within animations is equally important. The font choice and its animation can emphasize key messages or create visual interest. Using animated text to highlight specific words or phrases adds another layer of dynamism. Select fonts that are legible and complement the overall animation style. Avoid overcrowding text within the animation, ensuring it's easily readable even in motion.

In conclusion, Canva's animation tools provide an accessible and powerful way to elevate your graphic design. By understanding the fundamentals of animation, optimizing for platforms, and considering accessibility, you can transform static designs into engaging visuals that capture attention and leave a lasting impression. Experimentation is key to mastering these tools and finding the perfect animation style for your design needs. The simplicity of Canva's approach makes animation techniques easily attainable for anyone, regardless of prior experience, allowing you to significantly enhance your design projects with captivating movement and visual flair. Remember to always consider your target audience and the platform you're using when deciding on your animation style and complexity. Start with simple animations, gradually exploring more advanced techniques as you gain confidence and experience. The rewards—enhanced engagement, increased memorability, and a more professional finish to your designs—are well worth the effort.

Mastering Canvas Effects and Filters

Canva's extensive library of effects and filters provides a powerful arsenal for enhancing your designs, transforming ordinary visuals into something truly extraordinary. These tools allow you to quickly and easily alter the mood, style, and overall aesthetic of your creations, adding depth and complexity without requiring extensive design expertise. Mastering these tools unlocks a world of creative possibilities, enabling you to craft visually striking designs that capture attention and resonate with your audience.

Let's start by understanding the difference between effects and filters in Canva. While both modify the visual appearance of your design elements, they do so in distinct ways. Filters typically alter the overall color scheme, tone, and contrast of an image or design. They act as a global adjustment, impacting the entire element. Imagine applying a "vintage" filter; it might subtly desaturate colors, add a warm tone, and introduce a slight grain effect, creating a nostalgic feel across the entire image. Conversely, effects are generally more targeted and localized, applied to specific elements rather than the entire design. Effects can include shadows, glows, blur, and other modifications that change the appearance of individual components without significantly affecting the surrounding elements. For instance, you might apply a drop shadow effect to a text box to make it stand out from the background or add a subtle glow to a button to draw attention to it.

Canva offers a wide selection of filters, categorized for easier navigation. You'll find filters for various moods and styles, such as vintage, black and white, dramatic, and vibrant. Each filter provides a unique visual alteration, impacting color saturation, contrast, and overall tone. Experimenting with different filters is crucial to discovering the styles that best complement your designs. Remember that filters aren't always a one-size-fits-all solution. A filter that works beautifully on one image might not yield the same desirable effect on another. The success of a filter depends on factors such as the original image's composition, its color palette, and the desired aesthetic.

One effective strategy is to combine filters to create nuanced and layered effects. Start with a base filter that sets the overall tone, and then add another to subtly enhance or refine the effect. For instance, you might begin with a "vintage" filter to create a slightly aged feel, then add a "warming" filter to intensify the warmth and create a sun-drenched appearance. This layered approach allows for more precise control and creates a unique visual signature that distinguishes your work. Conversely, you can start with a dramatic filter to create a strong initial effect and then overlay a softer filter to reduce harshness and add subtle nuance.

Beyond simply selecting a filter from the pre-set options, Canva allows for manual adjustments. Most filters provide sliders that enable you to control the intensity of the effect. For instance, you can finely tune the level of saturation, contrast, or warmth, allowing for precise control over the final result. This flexibility is essential for creating subtle and tailored effects. Don't be afraid to experiment with different levels of intensity. A small adjustment can make a big difference, and slight variations can significantly impact the overall visual impact.

Now let's turn our attention to effects. Canva offers a multitude of effects, each capable of subtly or dramatically altering the appearance of individual design elements. These effects add depth, texture, and a sense of dimensionality to your designs, taking them beyond the flatness of simple images and text. Let's examine some of the commonly used effects and their applications.

The "Shadow" effect is one of the most versatile tools in Canva's arsenal. By adding a shadow to an element, you can create a sense of depth and separation from the background. You can adjust the shadow's color, blur, and distance, allowing for fine control over the final effect. A long, soft shadow can evoke a sense of distance and space, while a short, sharp shadow creates a more defined and distinct look. The shadow effect is invaluable for making text or images stand out, particularly when working with busy backgrounds. Consider experimenting with different shadow colors to match or complement your design's overall palette.

The "Glow" effect adds a luminous quality to elements, creating a sense of emphasis and importance. Similar to the shadow effect, you can adjust the glow's color, intensity, and size to fine-tune the effect. A subtle glow can enhance readability or subtly highlight an element without being overly distracting, while a more intense glow can grab attention and draw the viewer's eye. Consider using the glow effect sparingly, as overuse can lead to cluttered or overly busy designs.

The "Blur" effect is useful for creating a soft, dreamy quality or drawing attention to specific areas of your design. You can apply different blur techniques, ranging from a subtle softening to a complete out-of-focus effect. Blur can effectively reduce noise or distraction in an image, or it can be strategically used to create a sense of movement or depth. For example, a blurred background can help your main subject matter stand out.

Canva also provides effects that enhance the textures of elements. These effects can add grain, patterns, or other visual textures, adding a layer of complexity and visual interest. They can be particularly useful for creating a vintage or retro feel, or for mimicking the appearance of various materials like paper, fabric, or metal. Experimenting with different texture effects is an excellent way to find unique and unexpected ways to enhance your designs.

Combining effects and filters can unlock even greater creative potential. Imagine using a "vintage" filter to establish a retro tone, then adding a subtle glow effect to specific elements to draw attention to them, or adding a drop shadow effect to create a sense of depth. The possibilities are endless, and experimentation is key to mastering this technique. Don't be afraid to experiment with different combinations and see what you can create. Start with simple combinations and gradually experiment with more complex arrangements.

When combining effects and filters, consider the overall composition and visual balance of your design. Avoid overwhelming your designs with excessive effects or filters. Overuse can lead to a cluttered or visually jarring effect, undermining the overall aesthetic. Strive for a balance between enhancing the design and maintaining clarity and visual appeal.

Furthermore, consider the context in which your design will be used. A design intended for print may require different effects and filters than one designed for online use. Print designs often benefit from more subtle enhancements, while online designs can be more vibrant and attention-grabbing. The platform's limitations in color reproduction may also affect your choices. Always consider the platform's capabilities and limitations.

Finally, remember that practice is crucial to mastering Canva's effects and filters. Experimentation is key to discovering the optimal combinations and techniques that best suit your design style and the specific needs of your project. Don't be afraid to explore different approaches, try unexpected combinations, and learn from your mistakes. The more you experiment, the more confident and skilled you will become in using Canva's powerful design tools. The ability to create stunning and professional-looking designs using effects and filters is a significant advantage for any graphic designer. Mastering these features opens up a world of creative expression and allows you to elevate your projects to a new level. Remember to always consider the overall impact of your choices, aiming for designs that are not only visually appealing but also communicate effectively and resonate with your target audience.

Working with Custom Fonts and Branding

Up to this point, we've explored Canva's built-in features, delving into the versatile world of effects and filters. Now, let's elevate your designs further by harnessing the power of custom fonts and their crucial role in branding. While Canva offers a vast library of readily available fonts, incorporating your own custom fonts opens a world of possibilities, allowing you to create a unique and cohesive brand identity. This level of customization allows you to reflect your brand's personality and values in a way that pre-selected fonts simply cannot achieve.

Uploading and using your own fonts in Canva is surprisingly straightforward. First, you need to acquire the font files. These are usually downloaded from font marketplaces or provided by a designer. Common file types include .ttf (TrueType Font) and .otf (OpenType Font). Once downloaded, you can easily upload them to Canva. Navigate to the "Uploads" section in your Canva design, usually located in the left-hand navigation panel. Click on the "Uploads" tab and then select "Upload a file." Choose your font files from your computer's storage and Canva will efficiently upload them.

After successfully uploading the fonts, they will appear in your font list within the text editing tools. This is where the magic begins. You can now select your newly uploaded custom font from the dropdown menu alongside Canva's existing font library. Applying your chosen font to your text is simply a matter of selecting the text and choosing your custom font from the font selection menu. Now, your meticulously chosen typeface is ready to be used across all of your designs.

The ability to use your own fonts is a game changer for maintaining brand consistency. Consistent brand identity, including typeface choice, fosters recognition and trust with your audience. When viewers associate a specific font with a particular brand, a level of subconscious recognition is created, making your brand stand out amidst the visual noise of the internet and beyond. In the digital landscape, brand recognition is paramount for success.

Choosing the right custom font requires careful consideration. The font should reflect your brand's personality and values. A playful, hand-drawn script font might be ideal for a children's clothing line, while a bold sans-serif font might be more appropriate for a tech company. The font should not only be visually appealing but also legible and functional. Imagine the frustration of a potential customer struggling to decipher your contact information due to an illegible font. Choosing an aesthetically beautiful but virtually unreadable font could undermine your efforts to communicate effectively.

Consider the context in which your design will be used. A font that works well on a large display might appear cramped or blurry when printed on a business card. If you're designing for various mediums like posters, brochures, or online platforms, always test the readability and scale across various output formats. High-resolution screens can render fonts differently compared to print, so meticulous testing is crucial for ensuring consistency. This level of forethought ensures that your message remains clear and your brand identity remains consistent across the board.

Before diving into using custom fonts, you need to understand the legal implications involved. Not all fonts are free for commercial use. Many fonts available online come with specific licensing agreements that restrict their use. Carefully review the licensing agreement provided with the font before using it in your designs. Inexperienced designers are often unaware of the potentially significant legal implications of using unlicensed or inappropriately licensed fonts. Using a font without proper permission can result in copyright infringement, leading to legal action and significant financial penalties.

To avoid this, familiarize yourself with different licensing models, like free for personal use, open source, and commercial licenses. Each license dictates how the font can be used and often defines limitations on distribution, modification, or commercial application. Understanding these nuances is crucial to avoiding legal pitfalls and protecting both your business and the rights of the font creators. There are numerous online resources dedicated to understanding font licenses and ensuring that your font usage remains compliant.

Let's delve into some practical examples. Imagine a bakery wanting to design its packaging. They might opt for a friendly and slightly whimsical serif font to convey warmth and tradition, perhaps accented with a simpler sans-serif font for practical information. Contrastingly, a law firm might choose a classic and elegant serif font, suggesting trustworthiness and professionalism. The selection reflects not just aesthetic preferences but also the core values and targeted audience of each business.

The careful selection of fonts is directly linked to the overall design success. Font choice has a profound impact on the mood, atmosphere, and effectiveness of your design. A font conveys not just textual information but also a wealth of unspoken communicative cues. The interplay of typeface weight, style, and kerning significantly influences the visual perception and emotional response to your design. Consider how a thin, delicate font projects a different feel compared to a bold, assertive font. This selection has a considerable impact on your brand's narrative and how your message is received by your target audience.

Canva, despite its ease of use, does have some limitations when it comes to font usage. You might not be able to use every font file type, and certain advanced typographic features available in professional design software might not be present in Canva. This is where understanding your design objectives becomes crucial. If you require advanced typography features, you might want to design in dedicated software and then import the final graphics to Canva for further refinement. Knowing the boundaries of the platform empowers you to plan strategically and utilize Canva's strengths without facing unexpected limitations.

Beyond simply choosing a font, consider other typographic considerations. These include kerning (the space between individual letters), tracking (the space between words), and leading (the space between lines of text). These subtle adjustments can significantly improve the readability and overall aesthetic appeal of your design. In Canva, while automatic adjustments often suffice, you have a degree of manual control over these elements, allowing for fine-tuning to optimize legibility and visual harmony. Mastering these adjustments creates a higher level of polish and professionalism in your designs.

Once you've incorporated your custom fonts and are satisfied with the visual outcome, it's critical to preview your designs on different devices and platforms. How does the design look on a smartphone, tablet, or desktop? Are there any readability issues on a smaller screen? Addressing these variations ensures that the final product remains consistent and appealing across a wide range of viewing experiences. This step is frequently overlooked, but it ensures that your design remains impactful and legible regardless of the platform.

In conclusion, while Canva's built-in fonts are extensive, incorporating your custom fonts allows for a level of brand consistency and visual uniqueness that cannot be replicated. It reflects a higher level of professional design and adds a distinctive quality to your projects. However, remember the crucial importance of understanding font licensing and adhering to the legal guidelines. With thoughtful font selection and attention to typographic detail, you can create designs that effectively convey your brand's message and resonate with your target audience. Mastering the art of custom font integration in Canva empowers you to elevate your designs beyond the readily available, into a realm of personalized brand identity.

Exporting and Optimizing Designs for Different Platforms

Now that we've explored the power of custom fonts and their impact on brand consistency, let's shift our focus to the equally crucial aspect of exporting and optimizing your Canva designs. Creating a stunning design is only half the battle; ensuring it looks equally impressive across various platforms is the other. The way you export your design directly impacts its final appearance and functionality, so understanding the nuances of different file formats and optimization techniques is essential.

One of the first decisions you'll face is choosing the right file format. Canva offers several options, each with its own strengths and weaknesses. The most common choices are JPEG, PNG, and PDF. JPEG (Joint Photographic Experts Group) is a widely used format for photographs and images with smooth color gradations. It's a lossy format, meaning some image data is compressed away during the saving process to reduce file size. While this results in smaller files, it can also lead to some minor quality loss, especially noticeable with sharp edges or text. JPEGs are generally suitable for web use, where file size is often a limiting factor.

PNG (Portable Network Graphics) is a lossless format, preserving all image data during compression. This makes it ideal for images with sharp lines, text, and logos, ensuring crispness and clarity. However, PNG files are usually larger than JPEGs, which can impact loading times on websites. The transparency feature offered by PNGs is invaluable for designs containing transparent backgrounds or elements that need to seamlessly integrate with other visuals. This makes PNG the preferred format for logos, graphics with transparent sections, and designs intended for use on websites or applications requiring a transparent background.

PDF (Portable Document Format) is a versatile format designed for preserving the integrity of documents. It's particularly beneficial for designs intended for print, as it maintains the resolution and fidelity of the original design. PDF files are also ideal for designs that need to be shared across different platforms and devices, without the risk of formatting inconsistencies. Consider using PDF for brochures, presentations, posters, and any design needing consistent appearance regardless of the software or operating system used to view them.

Beyond choosing the right file format, optimizing the resolution is crucial for ensuring your designs look sharp and clear on different devices and platforms. Resolution refers to the number of pixels in an image. Higher resolution means more detail and clarity, but also a larger file size. When exporting for the web, you need to strike a balance between image quality and file size. Large files take longer to load, potentially frustrating users and negatively impacting your website's performance. For web designs, a resolution of 72 DPI (dots per inch) is generally sufficient. The web is primarily optimized for digital screens, which rarely require the high resolution needed for print.

Exporting for print requires a significantly higher resolution, typically 300 DPI or more. Print media, like brochures or posters, require a much greater level of detail to ensure the quality and sharpness of the final output. Lower resolution designs will appear blurry or pixelated when printed, undermining the professional appearance you're striving for. Always check your printer's specifications to determine the ideal resolution for optimal print quality. Investing the time to export with the correct resolution is an investment in the ultimate impact and quality of your print products.

The size of your final file is another crucial consideration, especially when sharing your designs online. Large files can take significantly longer to upload and download, causing frustration for both you and the recipient. Canva offers tools within the export settings to control file size and compression. Experiment with these settings to find the optimal balance between image quality and file size, keeping in mind the platform where you intend to use the design. Compressing images too aggressively can lead to noticeable quality loss, while excessively large files hinder easy sharing and efficient digital usage.

Before exporting your design, it's essential to conduct a thorough review. Check every detail meticulously, from text readability to image quality and color accuracy. Ensure that any embedded fonts or images are correctly incorporated and won't cause issues after exporting. This review step prevents potential errors that could only become apparent after the design is exported and is far less easily corrected. Identifying these problems beforehand saves time, effort, and potential embarrassment.

Let's consider some practical scenarios. Imagine you're designing a social media post. A JPEG file with a 72 DPI resolution is ideal. The smaller file size ensures rapid loading on various devices and platforms, enhancing user experience. If you're creating a high-resolution image for print, like a poster, a high-resolution PNG or a PDF file is necessary, to prevent quality loss during the print process. For your business website's logo, a PNG with transparency is the preferred format to ensure a crisp, clean logo on various backgrounds.

Remember to always test your designs on different devices and platforms before finalizing them. This ensures consistency and readability across the spectrum of possible viewer experiences. Check how the design appears on smartphones, tablets, and desktops, adjusting the resolution or file size as needed. This testing procedure highlights potential issues, ensuring a consistent visual experience regardless of the viewing platform. Inconsistencies only become apparent once the design is deployed, highlighting the importance of pre-emptive quality assurance.

Exporting and optimizing your designs isn't simply about choosing the right format and resolution. It's about understanding your audience and the context in which they'll experience your work. By meticulously considering these factors, you can ensure your carefully crafted designs look their best, regardless of the platform. This attention to detail transforms a good design into a great one, reaching its full potential and effectively engaging the intended audience. Mastering these skills elevates your designs from amateur to professional, leaving a lasting and positive impression on your viewers. The final stage of the design process, often overlooked, plays a vital role in ensuring that your hard work translates into a polished, successful design. Taking the time to optimize for different platforms demonstrates a commitment to excellence, leaving a more impactful lasting impression.

Creating a Professional Design Portfolio

Now that we've mastered the art of exporting and optimizing our Canva designs, let's turn our attention to showcasing our hard work: building a professional design portfolio. Your portfolio is your visual resume, a curated collection of your best work designed to impress potential clients or employers. It's the ultimate demonstration of your design skills, creativity, and ability to translate ideas into compelling visuals. Building a strong portfolio is a crucial step in establishing yourself as a professional graphic designer.

The first critical step is selecting the right projects to include. Don't simply throw every design you've ever created into your portfolio. Instead, focus on your strongest pieces— those that best exemplify your skills and the type of work you want to attract. Consider projects that highlight diverse design skills, showcasing your versatility. For example, include projects demonstrating your mastery of typography, color theory, and layout, along with projects demonstrating your proficiency in various design styles. Aim for a balance; you want to demonstrate a wide range of capabilities while also maintaining a cohesive brand identity throughout the portfolio.

Consider the narrative you want your portfolio to tell. What story are you communicating about your design capabilities? What types of clients or employers are you trying to attract? Each project selection should contribute to the overall story, enhancing the narrative of your design journey. For instance, a project showcasing your branding abilities would be different from a project that focuses on website design. The selection process shouldn't be arbitrary; it should align with your professional design goals and objectives.

Once you've selected your projects, the next step involves presenting them effectively. A visually appealing layout is essential. Think of your portfolio as a design project in itself. The arrangement of projects, the use of whitespace, and overall visual harmony should all contribute to a positive and professional impression. Consistency in terms of style and presentation is important. Consider using a consistent color palette, font family, and visual style across all pages. This creates a cohesive experience, subtly hinting at the attention to detail and design mastery you bring to your projects.

The visual presentation of your work requires careful consideration. Ensure that each design is well-lit and presented in high-resolution images. Avoid using low-quality screenshots or images with distracting backgrounds. If necessary, take high-quality photographs of printed work, ensuring that the image accurately captures the design's details. The visual quality of your portfolio directly reflects the quality of your work.

Each project should have a concise and informative description. Avoid lengthy, rambling explanations. Instead, focus on highlighting the key aspects of the project. Begin by clearly stating the project's goal or objective. Then briefly outline the challenges you faced and the solutions you implemented. Finally, highlight the results you achieved, emphasizing quantifiable achievements whenever possible. For instance, if you designed a website, highlight metrics such as increased user engagement or conversion rates. This demonstrates your analytical abilities alongside your creative skills.

For example, instead of writing "I designed a logo for a coffee shop," consider a more detailed description like: "Designed a logo for a new organic coffee shop, incorporating natural imagery and a modern typeface to attract a younger, health-conscious demographic. The logo's clean design, used consistently across their branding materials, led to a 15% increase in social media engagement within three months." This approach quantifies the impact of your design, making your achievements more compelling to viewers.

The choice of platform for your online portfolio is also crucial. Several options exist, each with its own advantages and disadvantages. Behance, Dribbble, and Instagram are popular platforms for showcasing creative work. These platforms allow you to build a community around your work, potentially leading to new collaborations and opportunities. However, these platforms often focus on individual projects, making it harder to present a cohesive portfolio narrative.

Conversely, building a self-hosted website provides greater control over your portfolio's design and content. This allows you to create a truly personalized presentation of your work, reflecting your personal style and brand identity. However, this requires additional technical skills or the investment in hiring a website developer. Carefully consider your technical skills and financial resources when selecting a platform. A well-structured, easy-to-navigate website can elevate your portfolio to a higher level, showcasing your professionalism and sophistication.

Remember that your portfolio is a living document. It should evolve as your skills and experience grow. Regularly update your portfolio with your latest projects and remove older or less impressive works. This demonstrates that you are actively growing as a designer and that you are committed to creating high-quality work. The act of regularly updating your portfolio itself is a significant statement; it underscores your commitment to ongoing professional development.

Consider also including a brief "About Me" section where you can introduce yourself and your design philosophy. This section adds a personal touch, connecting you with potential clients and employers on a more human level. Don't be afraid to showcase your personality and passions in this section. A well-written "About Me" section can make you more memorable, highlighting your distinct approach to graphic design.

Furthermore, consider adding a contact section, enabling potential clients or employers to easily reach you. Include your email address, phone number, and links to your social media profiles. Making it easy to connect is critical; you want to make it effortless for people who are impressed by your work to reach out and collaborate. This seamless integration between portfolio and contact information significantly improves the chances of securing new opportunities.

In conclusion, building a compelling design portfolio is an ongoing process, requiring careful planning and consistent effort. However, the investment is worthwhile. A well-crafted portfolio is an invaluable asset, enhancing your professional credibility and expanding your opportunities. By carefully selecting your best projects, presenting them effectively, and choosing the right platform, you can create a portfolio that truly showcases your design skills and helps you stand out in a competitive market. Remember, your portfolio is a reflection of you and your aspirations—so make it count. It's a powerful tool that enables you to present your capabilities effectively, attracting the attention of potential clients and employers alike. Treat your portfolio as a dynamic representation of your creative journey, continuously refining and updating it to reflect your growth as a designer. This commitment to excellence demonstrates your dedication to the profession, ensuring that your portfolio consistently leaves a lasting and positive impression.

Monetizing Your Design Skills

Now that you've meticulously crafted a portfolio that showcases your design prowess, it's time to explore the exciting possibilities of monetizing your Canva skills. The ability to create stunning visuals is a valuable asset in today's digital world, and numerous avenues exist for turning your passion into profit. This section will guide you through various strategies for transforming your design expertise into a sustainable income stream.

One of the most accessible and popular routes is freelancing. The gig economy offers a flexible and rewarding path for graphic designers. Platforms like Upwork, Fiverr, and Freelancer.com connect freelancers with clients seeking design services. These platforms provide a built-in marketplace, simplifying the process of finding projects and managing client interactions. However, competition can be fierce, so creating a compelling profile and showcasing your Canva skills through high-quality examples in your portfolio is crucial. Start by carefully examining the types of projects available on these platforms and tailoring your profile to match the specific needs of potential clients. Remember that clear communication and timely project delivery are vital to building a strong reputation and securing repeat business.

Beyond general freelancing platforms, consider networking within your local community. Many small businesses and entrepreneurs require graphic design services but lack the in-house expertise. Reaching out to local businesses directly—through networking events, online forums, or even simply by sending personalized emails—can lead to valuable local clients. This personalized approach allows for stronger client relationships, resulting in more consistent work and opportunities for long-term partnerships. Think about creating flyers or postcards to distribute locally, emphasizing the cost-effectiveness and convenience of your Canva-based services.

Expanding your reach online can also yield significant results. Consider creating a professional website or using platforms like Instagram and Behance to showcase your work and attract clients. A well-optimized website with clear pricing and a contact form can streamline the process of acquiring new projects. Remember to include testimonials from satisfied clients, further reinforcing your credibility and trustworthiness. Highlight your Canva expertise, emphasizing the efficiency and cost-effectiveness you bring to projects compared to traditional design software. This allows potential clients to clearly see the value proposition of your services. For example, you can promote your Canva proficiency by stating that you can deliver designs quickly and at a lower cost because of its user-friendly interface and extensive template library.

Another avenue for monetizing your Canva skills involves creating and selling design templates. Canva's template marketplace offers a direct route to reaching a large audience of potential buyers. By designing high-quality, versatile templates, you can generate passive income while sharing your creative talents with a broader community. Focus on identifying popular design trends and niches to maximize your sales potential. Conduct thorough keyword research to identify popular search terms, ensuring that your template titles and descriptions are optimized for discoverability. High-quality product photography, detailed descriptions, and positive customer reviews are essential components of successful template selling.

When creating your templates, consider the different needs and skill levels of your target audience. Offer various levels of customization, from simple color changes to more intricate design adjustments. The more versatile your templates, the wider their appeal and the greater their potential for generating income. Consider offering template bundles or packages to incentivize customers to buy multiple templates at once. This can significantly increase your average order value.

Beyond templates, you can also sell design services directly through your own website or social media channels. Creating visually appealing service pages is critical to presenting your offerings clearly and attracting clients. Highlight your experience, expertise, and the unique value you bring to clients. Consider offering various packages of design services, catering to different budget levels and project scopes. For instance, you might offer basic logo design packages, more comprehensive branding packages, and advanced website design packages. This tiered approach allows clients to choose a service that aligns with their needs and budget.

Setting competitive pricing is essential for attracting clients without underselling your skills. Research industry rates for similar services, considering your experience and the complexity of the projects you undertake. Start with a clear and concise pricing structure, easily accessible on your website or social media pages. Transparency in your pricing will establish trust with potential clients. Always clearly communicate what's included in each pricing tier to prevent misunderstandings and ensure client satisfaction. Remember that you are selling a valuable service, and your pricing should reflect the time, skills, and creativity involved in creating professional designs.

Marketing your services effectively is crucial for attracting clients and building a strong client base. Utilize social media platforms such as Instagram, Facebook, and Pinterest to showcase your work and engage with potential clients. Create visually engaging content, including behind-the-scenes glimpses of your design process, and share client testimonials to demonstrate your expertise and build credibility. Use relevant hashtags to increase the visibility of your posts, reaching a broader audience interested in your services. Consistent posting and engagement are essential for building a strong social media presence and attracting potential clients.

Beyond social media, explore other marketing strategies like content marketing, guest blogging, and participating in online design communities. Creating valuable content related to graphic design and Canva can establish you as an authority in your field and attract potential clients organically. Guest blogging on relevant websites allows you to reach a wider audience and increase your online visibility. Networking within online design communities can lead to collaborations, referrals, and new project opportunities. Remember to build relationships with other designers and businesses in your niche. This expands your network and generates opportunities for collaboration or referrals.

Managing projects effectively is essential for delivering high-quality work and maintaining positive client relationships. Establish clear communication channels from the outset, outlining project timelines, expectations, and deliverables. Use project management tools to track progress, communicate updates, and ensure timely completion. Consistent communication and regular updates keep clients informed and build trust, resulting in a smoother project workflow. Always ask for feedback throughout the process to make sure the client is satisfied with the direction the project is taking. This collaborative approach fosters strong client relationships.

Finally, always strive for continuous improvement. The graphic design landscape is constantly evolving, with new trends and tools emerging regularly. Investing in ongoing education and skills development will ensure you stay ahead of the curve and remain competitive in the market. Stay updated on the latest design trends, explore new Canva features, and continuously refine your skills to deliver exceptional results. This commitment to growth ensures your services remain relevant and valuable, attracting clients and leading to long-term success. Remember that your ability to adapt and innovate is crucial for sustained success in this dynamic field. By embracing continuous learning and consistently striving for excellence, you can build a thriving and successful graphic design business based on your Canva skills.

Staying Current with Canva Updates and Trends

The foundation of a successful graphic design career, particularly one built on Canva's capabilities, lies not only in mastering current tools but in consistently adapting to the ever-changing landscape of design trends and software updates. Canva, itself a dynamic platform, frequently introduces new features, templates, and functionalities, demanding ongoing learning and adaptation from its users. Ignoring these updates could mean missing out on valuable time-saving tools, innovative design options, and ultimately, a competitive edge in the market.

One of the most straightforward ways to stay abreast of Canva's updates is through the platform itself. Canva regularly announces new features and improvements through in-app notifications, email newsletters, and updates to their help center. Actively engaging with these communications ensures you're among the first to know about significant changes, allowing you to integrate them seamlessly into your workflow. Explore the "Help" section within the Canva interface; it's a treasure trove of information encompassing tutorials, troubleshooting guides, and announcements on new features. Don't just skim; dedicate time to understanding how each new tool or update can enhance your design process. Consider experimenting with these new features on personal projects to familiarize yourself with their functionality before incorporating them into client work.

Beyond the platform itself, a plethora of online resources are dedicated to covering Canva's updates and offering insightful tutorials. Numerous blogs and websites specialize in Canva tutorials and news. These resources often offer in-depth analyses of new features, providing practical examples and tips for their effective implementation. A simple online search for "Canva new features" or "Canva updates" will yield a wealth of information from various credible sources. Scrutinize the credibility of these sources. While many are reliable, always verify information against official Canva resources to ensure accuracy and avoid misinformation.

Online communities focused on Canva users are invaluable hubs of information and shared experience. Forums, social media groups (such as Facebook groups or Reddit communities), and online discussion boards provide a platform to interact with fellow Canva users, ask questions, share tips, and learn from others' experiences. Engage actively in these communities. Ask questions, offer assistance, and contribute to discussions. This reciprocal engagement not only helps you learn but also builds your professional network, potentially opening doors to collaborative opportunities or valuable mentorship.

Another powerful tool for staying updated is subscribing to relevant newsletters and podcasts. Many design blogs and industry publications offer newsletters specifically focused on Canva, graphic design trends, and related software updates. These newsletters often provide curated content, offering a concise summary of the most important developments in the field. Similarly, many podcasts feature interviews with graphic designers, discussions on current design trends, and reviews of new design tools, including Canva updates. Listen actively; jot down key points and consider how you can integrate the insights gained into your own work.

Staying current doesn't solely involve technical proficiency; it extends to understanding prevailing design trends. Design aesthetics evolve constantly, reflecting broader societal shifts and technological advancements. What's trendy today may be outdated tomorrow. Keeping a finger on the pulse of design trends is essential for creating visually appealing and marketable designs.

Design blogs and publications are excellent resources for staying informed about emerging trends. These blogs often feature articles analyzing current design styles, showcasing examples of exceptional work, and predicting future trends. Many of these publications also offer insights into the psychology of design, explaining why certain trends resonate with audiences and how designers can effectively leverage them. Actively read these publications; explore examples of successful designs; and analyze how these trends can be translated to your Canva projects. Pay attention to how different design elements, such as color palettes, typography, and imagery, are used to create impactful visuals.

Social media platforms such as Pinterest, Instagram, and Behance are valuable visual repositories of current design trends. These platforms provide a visual overview of what's popular in various design niches. Explore different hashtags and search terms related to your area of interest. Analyze the designs you encounter; identify recurring elements, and try to understand the reasons for their popularity. Consider creating mood boards on Pinterest to gather inspiration and organize your ideas based on emerging trends.

Participating in online courses and workshops can significantly boost your understanding of current design trends and techniques. Numerous platforms offer online courses on graphic design, often focusing on specific design software like Canva. These courses often cover a range of topics, from design fundamentals to advanced techniques, including insights into current trends and best practices. Some courses even provide personalized feedback, assisting you in refining your skills and applying design trends effectively.

Continuous learning should be considered a cornerstone of your graphic design journey. The field is ever-evolving, demanding constant adaptation and upskilling. Staying static risks obsolescence; proactive learning ensures continued relevance and success. Embrace online tutorials; attend webinars; and participate in design communities. These resources provide a continuous stream of knowledge, ensuring you're always equipped with the latest techniques and insights. Don't hesitate to experiment with new features and styles; view failures as learning opportunities; and celebrate successes as stepping stones towards further improvement. Your willingness to learn, adapt, and stay abreast of trends will significantly impact your ability to create cutting-edge designs and remain competitive in the dynamic field of graphic design. This dedication to continuous professional development is not merely a recommended practice; it's the essential ingredient for long-term success in a constantly evolving field. Consider investing a specific amount of time each week dedicated to learning and exploring new features, updates, and trends. This consistent commitment ensures that you remain a highly skilled and sought-after graphic designer. Remember, the skills you acquire today are the foundation for even greater success tomorrow. Staying ahead of the curve ensures that your designs consistently reflect the most current trends, establishing you as a forward-thinking and adaptable professional in the field.

Expanding Your Design Skills Beyond Canva

While Canva provides an excellent foundation for graphic design, mastering it alone won't unlock the full potential of your creative vision. The graphic design world is vast and diverse, and limiting yourself to a single tool, however powerful, would be akin to using only a single brush in a painter's arsenal. To truly flourish as a graphic designer, you need to expand your skillset beyond the confines of Canva, exploring other software, techniques, and approaches that will enrich your creative abilities and enhance your portfolio's versatility.

This expansion isn't about abandoning Canva; it's about supplementing it. Canva remains a valuable tool for quick projects, social media graphics, and initial design concepts. Think of it as your trusty sketchpad, where you can rapidly iterate ideas and experiment with layouts. However, to achieve truly polished, high-resolution outputs, and to explore certain design functionalities not readily available in Canva, you'll need to venture into the wider world of graphic design software.

One of the most prominent pathways to enhancing your design capabilities lies in exploring the Adobe Creative Suite. Adobe Photoshop and Illustrator, in particular, represent industry standards in raster and vector graphics editing, respectively. Photoshop is ideal for image manipulation, photo retouching, and creating highly detailed raster-based designs. This software empowers you to perform complex tasks like color correction, image compositing, and the creation of highly realistic digital paintings or photo manipulations – aspects that, while possible within Canva, are often significantly more challenging and less efficient.

Learning Photoshop requires a dedicated commitment to understanding its numerous tools and features. Fortunately, a wealth of online resources is readily available, including tutorials on YouTube, detailed courses on platforms like Udemy and Skillshare, and countless blog posts and articles offering step-by-step instructions. Start with the basics, focusing on essential functions such as layer management, selection tools, and blending modes. As your proficiency increases, gradually incorporate more advanced techniques like masking, retouching, and color grading. Remember that mastering Photoshop takes time and patience; celebrate small victories along the way and don't be discouraged by the initial learning curve. The reward of acquiring this powerful skill will significantly boost your design capabilities.

Illustrator, on the other hand, focuses on vector graphics, making it ideal for creating logos, illustrations, and scalable artwork. Vector graphics are composed of mathematical equations, allowing them to be resized without any loss of quality. This makes them perfect for projects requiring high-resolution output, such as print materials or large-format displays. Illustrator's pen tools, shape tools, and type manipulation options provide immense creative flexibility, enabling the creation of sophisticated illustrations and designs that are impossible to replicate effectively in Canva. Similarly to Photoshop, learning Illustrator necessitates a structured approach, starting with the fundamental tools and progressively mastering more complex functions. Abundant online tutorials and courses are available to guide you through this learning process.

Beyond the Adobe suite, other software options warrant exploration, depending on your specific design interests. Affinity Designer and Photo offer robust alternatives to Adobe's products, providing comparable functionality at a more affordable price point. Procreate, specifically designed for iPad, excels in digital painting and illustration, offering a unique and intuitive workflow. Figma, a collaborative design tool, is gaining significant traction in the field of UI/UX design, emphasizing teamwork and real-time collaboration. The choice of software depends on your individual needs and preferences. Consider experimenting with free trials or demo versions to determine which software best aligns with your design style and project requirements.

Expanding your skills also involves exploring diverse design techniques beyond the tools themselves. Consider delving into areas like typography, color theory, and visual communication principles. Understanding the nuances of typefaces, their impact on readability and aesthetics, and the effective use of spacing and hierarchy is crucial for creating visually impactful designs. Similarly, a strong grasp of color theory, encompassing color harmonies, palettes, and the psychological implications of color choice, is vital for communicating specific emotions or messages through your designs. Visual communication principles, such as the Gestalt principles, help you understand how people perceive and interpret visual information, enabling you to create more effective and engaging designs.

Numerous online resources cater to these aspects of design. Books on typography, color theory, and visual communication are readily available, both in print and digital formats. Online courses and workshops offer structured learning experiences, providing valuable insights into these key design principles. Moreover, actively analyzing the work of established designers – examining how they utilize typography, color, and visual elements to convey their message – can be incredibly beneficial. Pay attention to the details; understand the design choices made, and consider how you could incorporate these principles into your own projects.

Another critical aspect of expanding your design skillset lies in seeking feedback and engaging with the design community. Sharing your work online, through platforms like Behance or Dribbble, exposes you to constructive criticism and provides opportunities for networking with other designers. Actively seeking feedback from peers, mentors, or even potential clients is essential for identifying areas for improvement and refining your design process. Join online forums or attend design meetups; these events foster collaboration and provide opportunities to learn from others' experiences. Remember that even experienced designers continually seek feedback and engage in continuous learning; it's an integral part of professional growth.

Finally, building a strong design portfolio that showcases your versatility is paramount. As you expand your design skills beyond Canva, incorporate examples of work created using other software and demonstrating your proficiency in various design techniques. Your portfolio should reflect your expanded capabilities, showcasing your adaptability and the breadth of your creative skills. A diverse portfolio not only demonstrates your expertise but also makes you a more attractive candidate for potential clients or employers, setting you apart in the competitive graphic design landscape. Remember that your portfolio is a living document; continually update it to reflect your latest projects and skill development.

In conclusion, while Canva provides a valuable entry point into the world of graphic design, its capabilities are only a fraction of what's possible. By expanding your skills to include other software, mastering essential design principles, and actively engaging with the design community, you'll unlock a new level of creative potential and significantly enhance your career prospects. The journey is one of continuous learning and adaptation, but the rewards of a diverse and well-honed skillset are immeasurable in the ever-evolving field of graphic design. Embrace the challenge, explore the possibilities, and watch your design abilities flourish. Your commitment to continuous learning will be the key to unlocking your full creative potential and ensuring your long-term success.

Community and Networking in the Design World

The journey of a graphic designer extends far beyond mastering a single tool like Canva. While Canva serves as an excellent starting point, a vibrant and thriving design career requires active participation in the design community. Networking and collaboration are not just beneficial additions; they are essential ingredients for growth, learning, and success in this dynamic field. Think of your design journey as building a complex structure – Canva provides the foundation, but the community provides the support beams, the decorative elements, and the overall structural integrity that will allow your design career to reach new heights. Ignoring this aspect is like building a house without considering the surrounding environment and support structures. You need a strong network to thrive.

One of the most immediate ways to immerse yourself in the design community is through online platforms. Websites like Behance and Dribbble are more than just portfolios; they are bustling hubs of creative expression and professional networking. Behance, for instance, allows you to showcase your work in a visually compelling way, complete with detailed project descriptions and behind-the-scenes insights. The platform's comment section enables you to engage directly with viewers, receiving valuable feedback and critiques that can significantly refine your skills and creative vision. Moreover, Behance's organizational structure, which allows for categorization and exploration of various design disciplines, allows you to discover designers whose work resonates with yours, fostering a sense of community and shared passion. It's not simply about showcasing your own creations; it's about actively participating in discussions and engaging with other designers' work. Leave thoughtful comments, share insightful observations, and genuinely connect with other artists in the community. This active participation will greatly increase your visibility and chances of collaborative opportunities.

Dribbble, with its unique shot-sharing system and curated community, offers a different approach to online networking. It emphasizes the process of design, allowing you to share work in progress and receive immediate feedback. This platform is particularly beneficial for fostering creativity and exploring new ideas. The emphasis on visual exploration and rapid iteration allows for a dynamic exchange of concepts and a deeper understanding of different design approaches. Through its invitation-only system, Dribbble maintains a high level of quality and fosters a sense of exclusivity, which can translate into significant professional networking opportunities. Again, active participation is key. Commenting on others' work, offering constructive criticism, and participating in design challenges allows you to make genuine connections and expand your professional network. Don't be afraid to reach out to designers whose work you admire; a simple message expressing appreciation can often lead to valuable conversations and potential collaborations.

Beyond Behance and Dribbble, a myriad of other online platforms offer avenues for networking. LinkedIn, although a broader professional networking site, has a strong design community where you can connect with recruiters, potential clients, and other designers in your niche. Joining relevant groups and participating in industry discussions keeps you abreast of current trends and enables you to connect with like-minded professionals. Consider actively searching for groups related to specific design fields, such as UI/UX design, graphic design for branding, or motion graphics, to network with specialists in those areas. Remember to maintain a professional profile that accurately showcases your skills and experience, highlighting your most impactful projects and contributions.

Online forums specific to design software, such as those related to Adobe Creative Suite or Canva itself, provide excellent opportunities to seek technical assistance, share tips and tricks, and learn from the collective wisdom of the community. Asking thoughtful questions, offering help to others when possible, and participating in discussions about software updates or design challenges will cement your position within the community and expose you to a wide range of expertise. Don't hesitate to seek clarification or guidance; the design community is typically quite receptive to new members seeking knowledge and support. This collaborative environment can also lead to unexpected connections and collaborative projects.

Offline networking is equally crucial. Attending industry conferences, workshops, and meetups allows you to forge personal connections, engage in face-to-face discussions, and build rapport with other designers. These events offer invaluable opportunities to learn from industry leaders, explore new technologies and techniques, and discover emerging trends firsthand. Actively participate in discussions, engage with speakers, and exchange business cards – or, in today's digital world, connect via LinkedIn or other social media platforms. Networking events are not only about collecting business cards; they are about forming genuine connections and establishing long-term professional relationships. Remember to approach each conversation with genuine interest and a willingness to learn. Listen actively to what others have to say, and look for ways to contribute to the conversation, rather than solely focusing on self-promotion.

Beyond formal events, look for opportunities to connect with fellow designers in your local community. This might involve joining local design groups or attending workshops at art supply stores or community centers. These local connections can provide valuable support, collaboration opportunities, and a sense of belonging within a supportive design community. Building a strong local network can lead to opportunities for freelance work, mentorship, or simply a supportive environment for bouncing ideas off fellow artists. Remember, every connection is a potential opportunity.

Participating in design challenges and competitions offers a fantastic way to improve your skills, receive feedback from peers, and showcase your talents to a broader audience. Many online platforms host regular design challenges, providing opportunities to test your skills, experiment with new techniques, and gain recognition from experienced designers. These competitions not only boost your portfolio but also expose you to new design concepts and collaborative opportunities. Even if you don't win, the experience of participating, the feedback you receive, and the exposure to other designers' work can be incredibly valuable.

Mentorship plays a significant role in professional development. Seeking guidance from experienced designers can provide invaluable insights, constructive criticism, and practical advice. Many established designers are willing to mentor aspiring artists, offering invaluable guidance on navigating the design industry, refining your skills, and building your career. You can often find mentors through professional networks, online forums, or even by directly reaching out to designers whose work you admire. Be prepared to demonstrate your dedication and commitment to learning; a sincere interest in mentorship is crucial in securing guidance from experienced professionals. A positive mentoring relationship can drastically improve your understanding of the field, provide valuable connections, and accelerate your professional growth.

Finally, remember that networking is an ongoing process, not a one-time event. Regularly engage with the design community, participate in discussions, and actively cultivate relationships. This consistent engagement will not only enhance your skills and knowledge but also build a strong professional network that supports your growth and success in the graphic design world. Your network is your greatest asset; nurture it, expand it, and watch your career flourish alongside the growth of your creative community.

Acknowledgments

First and foremost, I extend my deepest gratitude to my
family and friends for their unwavering support and
encouragement throughout the writing process. Their
patience and understanding, especially during those late
nights fueled by caffeine and deadlines, were invaluable.
I am also grateful to the Canva team for creating such a
powerful and user-friendly design tool. Their continuous
innovation and commitment to empowering designers of all
levels have made this book possible.

Appendix

Glossary

This glossary defines key design terms used throughout the book:

Color Theory: The study of colors and how they mix, match, and create different effects.
Typography: The art and technique of arranging type to make written language legible, readable, and appealing.
Layout: The arrangement of elements on a page or screen.
RGB: A color model used to represent colors on a computer screen.
CMYK: A color model used for printing.
Kerning: Adjusting the space between individual letters.
Tracking: Adjusting the space between all letters in a block of text.
Leading: Adjusting the space between lines of text.

References

Author Biography

www.ingramcontent.com/pod-product-compliance
Lightning Source LLC
LaVergne TN
LVHW051343050326
832903LV00031B/3708